BLENDED
COACHING

BLENDED COACHING

Skills and Strategies
to Support
Principal Development

GARY BLOOM   **CLAIRE CASTAGNA**   **ELLEN MOIR**   **BETSY WARREN**

CORWIN PRESS
A SAGE Publications Company
Thousand Oaks, California

For information:

Corwin Press
A Sage Publications Company
2455 Teller Road
Thousand Oaks, California 91320
www.corwinpress.com

Sage Publications Ltd
1 Oliver's Yard
55 City Road
London EC1Y 1SP
United Kingdom

Sage Publications India Pvt. Ltd.
B-42, Panchsheel Enclave
Post Box 4109
New Delhi 110 017 India

Printed in the United States of America

Library of Congress Cataloging-in-Publication Data

Bloom, Gary, 1953-
Blended coaching : skills and strategies to support principal
development / Gary Bloom . . . [et al.]
    p. cm.
Includes bibliographical references and index.
ISBN 978-0-7619-3976-4 (cloth) — ISBN 978-0-7619-3977-1(pbk.)
   1. School principals—Handbooks, manuals, etc. 2. Educational leadership—Study and teaching—Handbooks, manuals, etc. 3. School management and organization—Handbooks, manuals, etc. I. Title.
LB2831.93.B56 2005
371.2'012—dc22   2005002286

This book is printed on acid-free paper.

       07   08   09   10 9 8 7 6 5 4

Acquisitions Editor:	Rachel Livsey
Editorial Assistant:	Phyllis Cappello
Production Editor:	Kristen Gibson
Copy Editor:	Diana Breti
Typesetter:	C&M Digitals (P) Ltd.
Indexer:	Naomi Linzer
Proofreader:	William Stoddard
Cover Designer:	Rose Storey

Contents

List of Tables and Figures

Figures

Tables

Preface

WELCOME TO BLENDED COACHING STRATEGIES: SKILLS AND STRATEGIES FOR DEVELOPING SCHOOL PRINCIPALS

Schools need principals and other leaders who are able to build communities of practice that will enable all students to succeed. These leaders have a keen ability to promote collegiality, support adult learning, and nurture teachers. They encourage all members of the school community—students, teachers, and parents—to do their best.

Principals are responsible for setting the tone at their schools. And yet, as is frequently the case with teachers, principals are typically given the keys to the building, a pat on the back, and expected to go forth and succeed. New principals often have little or no supervised work experience and only limited practical preparation. Veteran principals struggle with changing expectations and increasing demands. As the "boomer" generation of principals faces retirement, school districts must contend with a well-documented shortage of candidates who have been suitably prepared to assume leadership positions.

Recognizing the importance of quality site leadership, school districts and other institutions around the country are currently working to establish more effective models of support for new and veteran school leaders. Calls for such programs have been issued by many national and state organizations. The need is further substantiated by our work at the New Teacher Center (NTC) at the University of California, Santa Cruz, where we provide intensive support to first- and second-year principals, experienced principals, and new teachers and their mentors.

This book offers a fresh approach to professional development for principals and other school leaders. *Blended Coaching: Skills and Strategies to Support Principal Development* addresses several critical needs:

- The importance of sustained, stable, and effective site leadership for school improvement
- The increasingly severe shortage of qualified candidates for the principalship
- The inadequacy of traditional preservice and inservice programs
- The need for quality induction and professional development programs for principals that include a mentoring or coaching component

This book is about helping principals and other school leaders bring themselves and their schools to their highest potential—by clarifying and then achieving their goals. It is about teaching, showing, guiding, and working side by side with school leaders to help them improve their performance. We believe the subject we address is of interest to all who are concerned with school improvement, including supervisors and faculty in administration preservice programs, central office personnel seeking to improve the quality of site leadership, and individuals now serving as coaches or mentors to school leaders around the country.

Norma is the brand new principal of Río Dulce Elementary School. She's 32 years old and grew up in the community where she now works. She was a successful teacher for five years and served as a middle-school assistant principal for eight months before being tapped for the principalship at Río Dulce. She is bright, motivated, and very knowledgeable about teaching and learning. Two weeks into the school year, however, she finds herself struggling with an array of issues that threaten to overwhelm her.

The purpose of this book is to help you help principals like Norma meet the challenges they face, survive the rough spots, and thrive in the important work they do. By supporting Norma in her work, you help her make a difference for the teachers, staff, students, and families of Río Dulce School.

Perhaps you are another principal in Norma's district and you have been asked to serve as Norma's mentor. You might be a retiree brought in by the district to assist new principals, or an independent consultant hired to provide leadership training. We suggest you consider our approach to professional development for principals: leadership coaching through the application of *Blended Coaching Strategies.*

Through several dozen years of collective experience, the authors of this book have learned a great deal about successfully coaching teachers and principals. Our experience is informed by 15 years of research and fieldwork, mentoring teachers and principals in dozens of school districts across the country.

Rose is in her second year as principal of Elm School. The staff appreciates her knowledge of instruction and her support. Although she is highly regarded by her school community and recognized for her commitment and hard work, she describes herself as "burnt out." She is losing confidence in her ability as a principal and is frustrated by the long hours she devotes to her job and her school's slow progress. She fantasizes about quitting. Instead of giving up, however, she shares her fears with Raul, her coach, who has built a trusting relationship with her. Raul observes Rose interacting with staff in a variety of contexts and helps her become aware of the ways in which her desire to control and her misgivings about delegating responsibility have burdened her and disempowered others. Raul helps Rose develop new structures for delegation and set personal limits on the number of hours she will work and the responsibilities she will take on. As a result, Rose becomes more comfortable stating her expectations and supervising her staff. By the end of her second year, she feels as if she has emerged from a bad dream—the kind where you are unable to outrun the monster that's close on your heels. Her job as principal becomes manageable, her attitude turns positive, and she begins to look forward to her third year at Elm.

It is our hope that this book will bring you to a new understanding of the concept of coaching and how it applies to the care and nurturing of school leaders like Norma and Rose. Skilled coaching has helped both Norma and Rose to emerge as outstanding instructional leaders who have had a significant positive impact upon their students. It is our aim to help individuals and organizations to design and implement programs that provide the intensive, individualized, and focused professional development so sorely needed by school leaders like Norma and Rose.

We have organized our approach to coaching around three essential elements: *skills, strategies,* and *tools.* Coaches, no matter what their particular approach, must apply a variety of basic *skills.* These include building trust; listening, observing, and questioning; and giving feedback. Coaches must also learn a number of *strategies,* the fundamental game plans that underlie coaching practice. We have developed *Blended Coaching Strategies* as a model for their application. Coaches should also come to the table with *tools,* those practical resources that shape the coaching relationship and from which a coach can draw to provide feedback and meet the coachee's specific job-related needs. Each of these elements—skills, strategies, and tools—is addressed in this book.

Coaching is a complex art, and expert coaches typically bring years of informal mentoring and other experience to the process. Many coaches have training in a variety of communication and adult learning models, including peer and cognitive coaching. Even if you have this kind of rich background, we hope you will think of this book as an introduction to the profession of leadership coaching. We believe it is essential that you broaden your capability by participating in interactive training and by being part of an ongoing community of practice where you can continue to develop your coaching expertise in the company of like-minded colleagues.

In the pages that follow, we provide you with tools to help you master our approach to leadership coaching. **Narrative text** sets forth key concepts and linkages between them, providing research results and references where appropriate. **Reflective prompts** are interspersed throughout the text. We encourage you to journal as you work your way through this book, using these prompts as tools to trigger your assimilation of the material. We also suggest you complete the included **Exercises**, either individually or with coachees or colleagues. Finally, we have included a number of **Tools** in the Resources section of this book. We hope these will be useful to you in your coaching practice.

If we are to construct school leadership development programs that attend to the needs of adult learners through coaching and mentoring approaches, it is necessary to establish a coaching model that can be taught, implemented, and evaluated. The goal of this book is to share our model with you and to lay the groundwork for the creation of a professional community of leadership coaches prepared to meet the needs of principals and other school leaders.

Welcome to the new profession of school leadership coaching. We invite you to join with us in creating a vibrant community of practice dedicated to supporting school leaders. We value your feedback and we look forward to hearing about the contributions you and others will make to this important work.

Acknowledgments

We are indebted to the Noyce and Stupski Foundations for their recognition of the importance of school leadership and their support of our work in this area. We particularly wish to thank Ann Bowers, Sonya Lopes, Lisa Trygg, Ben Sanders, and Joyce and Larry Stupski, who have championed our work in their foundations and in the K–12 community. Karen Frison, Larry Huggins, Tomasita Villareal-Carman, and Dale Zevin provided input important to the development of some of the materials and concepts included in this book. Cheryll Greenwood Kinsley provided essential assistance in the preparation of the manuscript. A portion of Chapter 2 first appeared in the American Association of School Administrators journal *The School Administrator*. We appreciate AASA's support of our work and permission to include that text. The Association of California School Administrators has been a key partner, helping us to share this work with the field in California and beyond. The New Teacher Center at the University of California, Santa Cruz, has offered us fertile ground in which we could grow and develop new approaches to professional development for school leaders.

Most important, we wish to thank the many school leaders who have demonstrated their commitment to their students and their profession by opening themselves, their schools, and their districts to new possibilities through leadership coaching.

In addition to those mentioned above, the contributions of the following reviewers are gratefully acknowledged:

Paul G. Young
Principal
West Elementary School
Lancaster, OH

Sharon Jackson
Associate Commissioner
Texas Education Agency
Austin, TX

Carolee Hayes
Co-Director
Center for Cognitive Coaching
Highlands Ranch, CO

Kathleen Bocchino
Director of New Teacher Induction
New York City Department of Education
New York, NY

Jan Robertson
Assistant Dean
School of Education
University of Waikato
Hamilton, New Zealand

About the Authors

Gary Bloom is the lead author of *Blended Coaching: Skills and Strategies to Support Principal Development.* He currently serves as Associate Director of the New Teacher Center at University of California, Santa Cruz. Gary has 23 years of K–12 education experience, having served as a bilingual teacher, principal, director of curriculum, and assistant superintendent. He served as the superintendent of the Aromas-San Juan Unified School District, known for its innovative programs, such as graduation exhibitions, a teacher-led high school, and teacher peer review. Gary is a Kellogg National Fellow, adjunct faculty to San Jose State University's Educational Administration graduate program, and has consulted, trained, and presented on a variety of topics throughout the United States and in Latin America. He is the primary author of a number of professional development programs for leadership coaches and school principals. He has published articles in a variety of journals, most recently on the topics of teacher leadership, principal development, professional learning communities, new teacher support, and the appropriate use of technology.

Claire Castagna is a program director and outreach consultant for the New Teacher Center's administrator induction program, Coaching School Leaders to Attain Student Success. She has 28 years of experience in education as a bilingual teacher, bilingual program coordinator, assistant principal, and principal. Throughout her career, Claire has focused on implementing programs that ensure that second language learners achieve excellence. She has presented her work in second language literacy at TESOL and CABE conferences. As a principal, Claire led her school to a California Distinguished School Award and became a mentor principal for the Santa Cruz County Baldrige in Education Consortium. Since 2001, Claire has coached beginning principals as they learn to balance the daily demands of the principalship with their role as instructional leaders and change agents. She has collaborated in the development of CLASS as a model of support for beginning principals and leads the development of the Improving Student Achievement series of workshops for site administrators on standards based supervision.

Ellen Moir is executive director of the New Teacher Center at the University of California, Santa Cruz. Ellen has also served for 15 years as Director of the Santa Cruz New Teacher Project, a beginning teacher induction program that has supported more than 12,000 beginning teachers during the first two years of their careers. From 1985 to 2000, she was UCSC Director of Teacher Education. In 2003, Ellen received the California Council on Teacher Education Distinguished Teacher Educator Award. She has recently addressed issues of new teacher support at the conferences of the National Governor's Association, National Board for Professional Teacher Standards, American Educational Research Association, and National Staff Development Council. Recent journal publications include articles for *Educational Leadership, Journal of Staff Development, Teacher Education Quarterly,* and *Chief State School Officers Council Newsletter.* Ellen has authored several book chapters related to induction and produced video documentaries on teacher induction and bilingual education.

Betsy Warren has worked in the field of education for 30 years. As a classroom teacher she taught grades 6–12 in four states. She was a teacher leader active in both local and state levels of teacher association activities. After completing her master's degree in School Administration, she worked as district coordinator of curriculum and staff development. She went on to become a site-level administrator where, she confesses, she learned more about herself, schools, and systems than she ever imagined possible. Betsy currently serves as outreach coordinator for the New Teacher Center, working with the CLASS Team's New Administrator Project. She also presents professional development seminars for new and veteran administrators. Betsy is a recipient of the Women Leaders in Education Leadership Award and a recent nominee for the Excellence in Education Award sponsored by the Office of the Mayor of San Jose.

PART I

Leadership Coaching Skills

In Part I, we explore the foundations of coaching as a tool for the professional development of school leaders. We define coaching, and we tie the power of coaching to what we know about how adults learn. We examine the uniquely challenging role of the principal and touch on the complex set of knowledge and skills that principals must possess. We pay particular attention to emotional intelligence and cultural proficiency as prerequisites to success as a school leader. We make a case for leadership coaching as an effective approach for helping school leaders to develop these competencies.

All coaches, whether coaching fly fishermen, CEOs, or synchronized swimmers, use a set of universal basic skills, such as trust building, listening, observing, questioning, and giving feedback. We explore these foundational coaching skills in the balance of Part I.

1

What Is Coaching?

"Coaching" is one of those words that is commonly understood but only vaguely defined. The *Oxford English Dictionary* devotes more than a page to the word coach, first used in the 15th century to describe a four-wheeled covered wagon used by royalty. In the 17th century the word morphed from a noun describing a carriage into one denoting "a private tutor who prepares a candidate for an examination."

> *A coach is someone who (1) sees what others may not see through the high quality of his or her attention or listening, (2) is in the position to step back (or invite participants to step back) from the situation so that they have enough distance from it to get some perspective, (3) helps people see the difference between their intentions and their thinking or actions, and (4) helps people cut through patterns of illusion and self-deception caused by defensive thinking and behavior.*
>
> Robert Hargrove, author of *Masterful Coaching*

Today we coach teams, we coach players, we coach our kids, and we coach our employees. There are birth coaches, executive coaches, and life coaches. In fact, tens of thousands of groups and individuals offer coaching services. Hundreds of organizations will train you to be a coach, and dozens more will certify you once you're trained. You can find many titles related to coaching at your local bookstore, including *Coaching and Mentoring for Dummies* (Brounstein, 2000). Coaching is all the rage, yet it enjoys no common definition, and little research has been done on its efficacy.

There are, however, commonalities that apply across the many and varied approaches to coaching, even as it is considered from a number of different viewpoints.

> *The coach's main role deals with expanding the ability to see contexts, rather than supplying content. The person being coached then sees new ways to utilize existing skills.*
>
> Julio Olalla, coach and trainer

> *The most effective way to forge a winning team is to call on the players' need to connect with something larger than themselves. . . . I've discovered that when you free players to use all their resources— mental, physical, and spiritual—an interesting shift in awareness occurs. When players practice what is known as mindfulness—simply paying attention to what's actually happening—not only do they play better and win more, they also become more attuned with each other.*
>
> Phil Jackson, basketball coach and author of *Sacred Hoops*

> *Start measuring your work by the optimism and self-sufficiency you leave behind.*
>
> Peter Block, author of *Flawless Consulting*

> *A coach is someone who tells you what you don't want to hear so that you can see what you don't want to see so that you can be what you've always wanted to be.*
>
> Tom Landry, football coach

> *What coaching does is to expand the space of possibilities that someone is—an expansion that requires an external intervention (coaching) to take place. Coaching allows the coachee to observe oneself as a self, to acknowledge the narrowness and limitations of that self, and to expand that self beyond its boundaries, beyond the horizon of possibilities available to the coachee's own intervention.*
>
> Rafael Echeverría, author of *The Art of Ontological Coaching*

Reflection: Based on the quotes you've encountered in this section, what would you say are the key elements of coaching? What knowledge and skills would a leadership coach need to possess?

We consider coaching to be *the practice of providing deliberate support to another individual to help him/her to clarify and/or to achieve goals.* This generic definition applies in many different settings—and in some of them, the label "coach" is never used!

REFLECTING ON THE FLIGHT INSTRUCTOR AS "COACH"

I learned to fly airplanes a few years ago. In many ways, this was the toughest learning challenge I have ever taken on. The learning process had many dimensions. There were the cognitive challenges of learning a new set of theories, rules, and procedures. There were the physical challenges of mastering a new set of motor and perceptual skills. There were the emotional challenges of overcoming the stress and fear I often experienced while at the controls of a small plane.

The cognitive aspects of flying were easy for me to learn and were mostly self-taught. To get a pilot's license you have to master airspace regulations, navigation, weather, and many other things, some vital, some trivial. In order to prepare for the Federal Aviation Administration written examination, I studied a text, listened to audiotapes, and practiced with test preparation software. I scored 98 percent on the written exam. As proud as this 40-something was of his score, he was far short of being a pilot.

The real work of learning to fly takes place in the company of a Certified Flight Instructor (CFI). This is a one-on-one relationship. From the first lesson, the student sits in the pilot's seat, the CFI alongside. A CFI draws upon a variety of strategies. Typically, new maneuvers are explained by the CFI, sometimes demonstrated, and then attempted by the student with the CFI ever ready to intervene. The CFI draws the student's attention to the indicators, the data sources that measure successful completion of the maneuver. For example, in completing a steep turn, a pilot is expected to maintain a bank angle of approximately 45°, not gain or lose altitude, and roll out of the 360° turn flying in the same direction as when the turn was started. The first time a student makes a steep turn, the CFI talks the student through the maneuver, telling him when to pull or push on the yoke and when to roll out of the turn. After a few rounds of "guided practice," a student should know the effects of his inputs and should be able to identify, on his own, the reasons for an unwanted altitude gain or a failure to maintain heading. Establish trust, demonstrate competence, observe the student pilot, and provide feedback—this is the work of a CFI.

But it is not this simple. Flying is a high-stakes business; small mistakes can lead to fatal consequences. When a CFI certifies that a student is ready to take the practical flight test, he or she is attesting to that student's capacity to take friends and family safely aloft, alone, into the wild blue yonder in a flimsy assembly of aluminum and steel.

When I had a panic attack early in my flight instruction and wanted to get on the ground immediately, my flight instructor complied. He also insisted, after a bitter cup of hours-old coffee, that we go up again. He asked that I relax while he ran through a series of stalls, killed the engine, and brought the plane down to a safe and quiet landing.

When I forgot to retract the plane's flaps at takeoff, resulting in a dangerously sluggish performance, he did not say a thing. When I turned to him and asked if something might be wrong, he suggested that I look at the plane's controls. I never attempted to take off again without checking the flap lever.

When, in my CFI's judgment, I was ready to fly solo, he stepped out of the plane and sent me off, linked to him only by a scratchy radio. When I was ready to fly my first cross-country flight, he reviewed my planning and released me for the trip. He was at the other end of the phone when I called to announce that I had made it back alive.

My experience learning to fly has shaped my conception of adult coaching. I suggest that we think of the Certified Flight Instructor as we develop a model of coaching. Here are some of the characteristics of the CFI's role and practice that also apply to leadership coaching:

- The CFI's job is goal-oriented: to prepare pilots to meet a set of well-articulated performance standards.
- The CFI works one-on-one with students, designing lessons and activities around individual needs.
- At times, the CFI provides direct instruction, explaining, demonstrating, and walking students through maneuvers.
- At times, the CFI observes while a student completes maneuvers independently, for the purpose of gathering data and proving feedback and to assess and build the student's capacity to complete maneuvers without a CFI alongside.
- A CFI seeks assurance that a new pilot is able to make high-stakes decisions and can respond to unexpected events safely and independently. To this end, CFIs use both simulations and the observation of performance in real situations as coaching and assessment tools.
- CFIs attend not only to skill but also to perception and emotion. They teach pilots which instruments and feelings to trust, and which to ignore. They help pilots learn to "fly the plane," ignoring distraction and emotion. They attend to the stress and fear that often accompany flight instruction.

I don't know which is more high stakes or unforgiving, flying a small plane or leading a school. I know that in both cases, the support of a CFI—or a coach—can make the difference between going places or "crashing and burning" when you're in that pilot's seat—or occupying the principal's chair—alone.

OUR DEFINITION OF COACHING

Coaching has been embraced by the private sector because it is a proven strategy for increasing the productivity and effectiveness of managers and executive leaders. As a means of providing deliberate support to clarify and achieve goals, coaching is also well suited to the needs of adult learners in the public sector. In *Why Can't We Get it Right?: Professional Development in Our Schools*, Marsha Speck and Caroll Knipe outline a number of research findings regarding adult learning that help to explain the success of coaching:

> Adults will commit to learning when they believe that the objectives are realistic and important for their personal and professional needs. They need to see that what they learn through professional development is applicable to their day-to-day activities and problems.
>
> Adults want to be the origin of their own learning and should therefore have some control over the what, who, how, why, when, and where of their learning.
>
> Adults need direct, concrete experiences for applying what they have learned to their work.
>
> Adult learners do not automatically transfer learning into daily practice. Coaching and other kinds of follow-up support are needed so that the learning is sustained.
>
> Adults need feedback on the results of their efforts.
>
> Adult learners come to the learning process with self-direction and a wide range of previous experiences, knowledge, interests, and competencies. (p. 109)

Direct, job-embedded coaching on a one-to-one basis responds to each of these characteristics of adult learners, whether they lead schools or private enterprises. Effective leadership coaching incorporates a number of key elements:

The coach constructs a relationship based upon trust and permission. True coaching cannot take place in the absence of a trusting relationship. The coachee must be willing to participate in the process—to learn, to grow, and to change in fundamental ways—and feel safe enough to open up and show vulnerability around the most sensitive issues of professional practice. It is the coach's responsibility to encourage this by working continually to build trust and permission. While these dynamic characteristics of the coaching relationship may fluctuate from one instance to the next, they should deepen and strengthen over time.

The coach serves as a different observer of the coachee and the context. One of the most important assets brought by a coach to the coaching relationship is fresh perspective. A coach provides the coachee with data and feedback about the coachee's behavior and the specific situation that may lead to new ways of acting. A golf pro, for example, may help a client make major improvements by pointing out what seem to be minor distinctions in the way the client holds a club. A leadership coach might use a 360° survey instrument to help a principal recognize that he or she is perceived as unfair because of the ways in which he or she interacts with some staff members.

The coach and coachee recognize that problems and needs are valued learning opportunities. It was Michael Fullan who penned the words, "problems are our friends" (1993, p. 21). Every problem presents an opportunity to learn and to grow by recognizing systemic issues that, if addressed, can lead to significant improvements. In the coaching process, problems and needs are sought out and embraced. This concept is at the heart of most coaching interactions.

The coach must be prepared to apply a variety of coaching skills *as appropriate to the context and needs of the coachee.* Effective coaches must master a number of fundamental skills, including listening, paraphrasing, questioning, and assessing the specific needs and contexts of the coachee.

The coach must be prepared to apply a variety of coaching strategies *as appropriate to the context and needs of the coachee.* Effective coaches often use multiple strategies during the course of any given coaching session. The coach may play a *facilitative* role, guiding the coachee to learning through the use of feedback and reflective questions. At other times, the coach might play an *instructional* role and provide expert information, advice, and resources. We call this approach *Blended Coaching Strategies* and believe its use is the foundation of an effective leadership coaching practice.

The coach is fully present for and committed to the coachee. A coaching relationship is unlike most other human relationships in the degree to which the coach attends to the coachee. Some coaches describe coaching as entering an altered state, a unique place where all of their experience, skill, and awareness is focused upon one other human being. The coaching relationship is all about the coachee and helping the coachee achieve specific goals. If you watch a videotape of a coaching session with the sound turned off, you will have no trouble distinguishing the coach from the coachee. A skilled coach directs all attention to the coachee and listens on multiple levels.

The coach provides emotional support to the coachee. Many leadership positions—including those of school leaders—are isolated and emotionally challenging. It is an important role of the coach to provide emotional support, offer encouragement, and help the leader maintain motivation and focus.

The coach maintains a fundamental commitment to organizational goals as agreed to by the coachee, and appropriately pushes the coachee to attain them. Although it results in more positive feelings about oneself and one's position, coaching is not intended merely to make leaders feel good, or help them be popular, or ensure that they survive in their jobs. Coaching instead is directed to the attainment of consensual goals. In the case of school leaders, this means helping them make a positive difference for the students at their sites. An effective coach always looks beyond and beneath any presenting problem, issue, or need, in order to find opportunities for growth and action that will help the coachee establish goals and make plans to achieve them. The coach also holds the coachee accountable to move forward with those plans.

The coach practices in an ethical manner. Professional ethics are critically important in coaching. Careers often hang in the balance, and high-stakes, rough-and-tumble politics sometimes come into play. Coaches must commit to confidentiality. They must carefully and explicitly negotiate their relationships with their coachees' supervisors. They must also be sensitive to and disclose promptly any personal biases, relationships, and histories that might impact their coaching, and they must comply with their agreements with their coachees and other clients.

WHAT COACHING *ISN'T*

In order to clarify the concept of coaching, it's useful to consider what coaching is *not*, and to review some of the practices that are sometimes confused with it.

Coaching is not training. Coaching addresses the needs of the individual rather than conveying a particular curriculum. While coaching can and often does support training activities, training is top-down and centered on content. Coaching, by contrast, is centered on context and designed to respond to the needs of the individual learner.

Coaching is not mentoring, although effective mentors use coaching skills and strategies. The terms *coach* and *mentor* are sometimes used interchangeably. For the purposes of our work, however, we define a mentor as an organizational insider who is a senior expert and supports a novice.

A coach is typically from outside the organization and is not necessarily senior—in age or depth of related professional experience—to the coachee. In our experience, novice principals benefit from having both a mentor *and* a coach. A mentor might be that veteran principal across town whom a novice can call to find out what procedures to follow to get her building painted, or how to work productively with the union representative, or whether she really needs to attend the upcoming meeting at the district office. Mentors can show newcomers the ropes in a number of situations. A coach, on the other hand, provides continuing support that is safe and confidential and has as its goal the nurturing of significant personal, professional, and institutional growth through a process that unfolds over time. A coach brings an outside perspective and has no stake in the status quo in an organization. Coaching is a professional practice; mentoring is typically voluntary and informal.

Coaching is not supervision, but effective supervisors coach a lot. There are distinct differences between the roles of coach and supervisor. A supervisor has the authority to give direction; a coach does not. A supervisor has an explicit role in determining a subordinate's employment status; a coach does not. A supervisor may be obliged to report on an individual's progress and problems to a superintendent or school board, while a coach can assure a coachee of confidentiality. A supervisor may have influence over the context an individual works in and the resources available to that individual; a coach does not. However, effective supervisors use coaching skills and strategies most of the time with their supervisees (and therefore have something to gain by applying the strategies and skills outlined in this book) and understand that most of the time their role is the same as that of a coach: to nurture growth in their subordinates.

Coaching is not therapy. An effective coach uses many of the same skills and strategies used by therapists. However, therapy focuses on the individual's psychological function, while coaching focuses on the accomplishment of professional goals. Therapy involves understanding an individual's past; coaching helps the individual change an organization's future. Therapy often treats issues of individual dysfunction or pathology; coaching occurs within the boundaries of normal professional issues. It is important that coaches be aware of these boundaries; while they do not aspire to the role of therapist, coaches should be prepared to suggest that coachees seek additional help if personal situations warrant.

LEADERSHIP COACHING FOR SCHOOL LEADERS

Effective school leadership coaching derives from consideration and thoughtful application of each of these elements: what coaching is, and what it is not.

School leaders are accomplished individual adult learners who are goal oriented and have very diverse needs. They are often expert in pedagogy and tend to resent and reject poorly designed and delivered professional development. However, they are likely to embrace effective coaching.

In our work around the country, we have asked hundreds of principals how they acquired the many skills and the broad knowledge essential to their jobs: in the teaching role, in preservice and inservice programs, through life experience, or on the job? They report that their most important learning takes place on the job—and note that preservice programs are among the *least* significant sources of preparation for the principalship. This is supported by a recent survey conducted by Public Agenda, in which 80 percent of superintendents and 69 percent of principals reported that graduate programs do not meet the needs of today's school leaders (Farkas, Johnson, Duffett, & Foleno, 2001). This may be attributable more to the complex nature of the principalship than to the quality of preservice programs.

It's hard out there in the landscape of school leadership. It can be brutal and lonely work. Principals often feel vulnerable and insecure. Our research tells us that their outlook and attitudes about their profession run through cycles ranging from desperation to optimism. It is no surprise, then, that principals frequently turn to their coaches for empathy and reassurance in addition to professional support.

We do not believe that coaches should serve their coachees simply as unquestioning cheerleaders. However, the coaching relationship will be strengthened if the coach communicates confidence in the coachee and if the coach recognizes that an appropriate element of her role is to convey enthusiasm for the coachee, for the coaching process, and for the work of school leadership.

Because a successful coaching relationship is based on trust and rapport, coachees believe in and respect their coaches. When a coach expresses confidence in a coachee, it has a significant impact on the coachee's outlook and performance—an impact that should not be underestimated. Indeed, an important part of the coach's role is to help coachees build and maintain self-confidence and commitment to their jobs. There are times when the most helpful thing a coach can do is lead the coachee through an inventory of the things that are going right and make note of the coachee's strengths. On some occasions, a coach can provide a great service by simply pointing out that the coachee's problems are not unique and offering assurances that they will be overcome. This, of course, is accomplished without a trace of dismissiveness or discounting the nature or seriousness of the problem.

Implicit in the relationship between a coach and coachee is the agreement by which the pair has set goals and in which each party has given certain permissions to the other. We suggest that fairly early in the relationship, as trust and rapport are being built, the coach and coachee have a conversation in which each outlines his or her expectations. Included in the conversation should be considerations such as:

- Developing a shared understanding of coaching
- Clarifying specific goals and focus areas for the coachee's professional growth
- Confirming confidentiality
- Establishing frequency of meetings
- Identifying means of communication
- Affirming commitments to openness
- Outlining activities to be observed and mechanisms for data gathering
- Discussing relationships and communication with supervisors
- Devising mechanisms for reevaluating and revising the relationship

Resource B at the end of this book contains an information sheet titled Making the Most of Coaching, developed to provide new coachees with a straightforward explanation of the coaching process. Also included is a sample agreement spelling out basic expectations, to be signed by all parties in a coaching relationship.

2

Meeting the Challenges of the Principalship

Principals are expected to possess educational expertise; to manage large organizations with complex programs, staffing, and budgets; and to work in a politically charged environment with constituencies that include elected officials, bus drivers, recent immigrants, union representatives, parents, novice teachers, business managers, lawyers, and five-year-olds.

If you're a principal, chances are these scenarios sound familiar.

It's your goal to spend 40 percent of your time in classrooms, but there are "discipline problems" lined up outside your door and a textbook order is overdue at the district office.

Your union building representative wants to meet with you because you have exceeded the number of allowable staff meeting minutes this month in your effort to organize English as a Second Language instruction at your site.

You have received an e-mail from the superintendent asking you to respond to accusations of racial bias in your staffing decisions.

If nothing changes, up to 40 percent of your students could fail the upcoming high school exit exam and be in danger of not receiving diplomas next spring.

Our leadership coaching work has taught us that principals face a set of common challenges. Each of these can be tied to standards such as those set by the Interstate School Leaders Licensure Consortium (ISLLC), and each draws upon a broad set of skills, abilities, and knowledge (ISLLC, 1996). To at least some degree, preservice programs do not or cannot provide adequate preparation in all of these areas. They simply cannot prepare candidates adequately for a job as difficult and complex as the principalship, unless they offer long-term preparation that places novices in highly structured internships with master principals. In addition, as demands and expectations change, even experienced principals need support.

Our formal research on leadership coaching has followed more than 60 principals through surveys and interviews and 10 principals through intensive case studies. This research has built our understanding of the challenges faced by today's principals. We have divided these challenges into three categories. The first category, professional knowledge and skills, includes the broad range of responsibilities and competencies that are outlined in the ISLLC standards. We highlight two additional categories, categories that are woven into ISLLC but that merit more direct attention, emotional intelligence and cultural proficiency. Our research and experience tell us that emotional intelligence and cultural proficiency are essential to school leadership, neglected as areas of focus in preparation and professional development programs, and primary focus areas for leadership coaching.

Reflection: What is your vision of the model principal, and what might be the key areas in which a coach can support a principal in embodying that vision?

PROFESSIONAL KNOWLEDGE AND SKILLS

The ISLLC Standards call for principals to have knowledge and understanding in 43 areas, ranging from "principles and issues relating to school safety and security" to "models and strategies of change and conflict resolution as applied to the larger political, social, cultural and economic contexts of schooling . . . global issues and forces affecting teaching and learning, the philosophy and history of education, community relations and marketing strategies and processes, measurement, evaluation and assessment, and systems theory." The Standards list 93 "performances" for which a school administrator should be held responsible. These range from the daunting and global, such as "effective communication skills are used," to the daunting and technical: "curriculum decisions are based on research, expertise of teachers, and the recommendations of learned societies." Principals are called upon to maintain "ongoing dialogue with representatives of diverse community groups," embrace "human resource functions that support the attainment of school goals," and exhibit the ability to communicate the vision and mission of the school "through the use of symbols, ceremonies, stories, and similar activities." They are further charged with involving "stakeholders in management processes" and establishing "high-quality standards, expectations, and performances" (ISLLC, 1996, pp. 10–21).

The ISLLC Standards present a vision of the principal as an instructional leader. They suggest that effective principals build communities of practice around a passionate commitment to student achievement, equity, and professionalism. School leadership coaching is designed to support the realization of this ambitious vision of the principalship.

The principalship is about complex work that cannot be mastered in the abstract. Much of what must be learned can be introduced in the classroom, but it is not likely to be learned well until a genuine need presents itself. Job-embedded, just-in-time learning—taking place when it addresses an immediate need and intended to be applied immediately—provides the adult learner with a reason to develop new knowledge and skills and the opportunity to apply them to the real world. It is in this context that a coach can be a powerful teacher.

In our experience, principals, especially novices, tend to need assistance in developing professional knowledge and skills in many areas, particularly in time management, delegation, staff supervision, meeting design and facilitation, budget management, categorical programs, data gathering and analysis, best practices in instruction, and leading change processes. Coaches need to be prepared in each of these areas in order to serve as teachers and resources to their principal coachees.

Here are two examples of situations in which leadership coaches have been able to assist their coachees in dealing with challenges requiring professional knowledge and skills aligned with ISLLC Standards:

ISLLC Standard 2 charges principals with responsibility for "advocating, nurturing, and sustaining a school culture and instructional program conducive to student learning and professional growth." Among other things, a school leader is expected to have knowledge of "curriculum design, implementation, evaluation and refinement" and "principles of effective instruction." A principal is expected to "facilitate processes and engage in activities ensuring that . . . barriers to student learning are identified, clarified and addressed and there is a culture of high expectations for self, student and staff performance" (ISLLC, pp. 12–13).

Adam was the second-year principal at Culver Middle School. The school had a good reputation and overall student achievement was perceived to be satisfactory. Adam's coach, Sylvia, led him through a process of examining and disaggregating a variety of student achievement data. Together they identified a small group of students who appeared to be falling through the cracks. These were English Language Learners (ELLs) who were advanced enough to be mainstreamed but not yet performing at grade level. Adam and Sylvia made numerous classroom visits focusing on the experiences of these particular students. Adam came to the conclusion that the unique needs of these students were not being addressed. They were often left to flounder without individual support, and their troubles went unnoticed because they were typically compliant and quiet. Sylvia helped Adam learn about best practices in meeting the needs of ELLs in middle schools by sharing articles with him and by arranging for him to visit model programs. Sylvia supported Adam in establishing a process with staff to examine student data and to learn, implement, and monitor new instructional approaches.

ISLLC Standard 3 requires that administrators "ensure the management of the organization, operations and resources for a safe, efficient, and effective learning environment." They must have knowledge of "human resources management" and "legal issues impacting school operations." The administrator is expected to facilitate processes and engage in activities to ensure that "collective bargaining agreements are effectively managed" and "human resource functions support the attainment of school goals" (ISLLC, pp. 14–15).

Marie was an experienced principal, recently transferred to Prairie High School from another high school in the same district. A traditionalist who was more comfortable as a manager than as an instructional leader, Marie found herself in a high school where teaching was done behind closed doors and where there had been little administrator presence in classrooms. Marie's new superintendent had made it clear that she expected principals to make instructional leadership their priority, and had provided all principals with coaching support. Marie's superintendent had asked that she work with her coach to get into classrooms and to shift the culture of the school from one focused upon maintaining tradition to one focused on teaching and learning. Marie did not know how she could make the time to get into classrooms or what processes to use to communicate with teachers about instructional issues and she feared a backlash from union leadership. Marie's coach, Alana, supported her in conducting an audit of the school's operations, with the goal of positioning operational support to free Marie and her assistant principals to spend more time on instruction. Marie and Alana reviewed the district's teacher contract and evaluation procedures and met with site union leadership to lay the groundwork for implementing a more thoughtful approach to supervision consistent with the negotiated agreement. Alana shared new tools with Marie for teacher supervision and support, including the examination of student work and achievement data and classroom quick-visits. Alana observed Marie using these tools and conferencing with teachers and gave her feedback all along the way.

ISSUES OF EMOTIONAL INTELLIGENCE

As important as professional knowledge and skills are, it is no secret that school leaders often fail not because they lack brains, determination, knowledge, or skills, but because of what is often characterized as "style" or "people skills." *Emotional Intelligence* (EI) is the term Daniel Goleman associates with this set of elusive competencies and dispositions that don't show up in most preservice programs. Goleman cites his own research and the work of others in arguing that EI has at least as much to do with on-the-job success as cognitive intelligence and technical expertise. He defines EI as "the capacity for recognizing our own feelings and those of others, for motivating ourselves, and for managing emotions well in ourselves and in our relationships" (Goleman, 1998, p. 317).

Few jobs present as many challenges to an individual's EI as the principalship. An effective principal must confront a broad spectrum of educational and management issues while building and maintaining relationships with multiple constituencies. The principal is expected to lead change processes in highly politicized and conservative institutions. No wonder, then, that most principals who leave their positions do so for reasons more related to EI than to their knowledge of reading programs or their ability to build a master schedule.

While principals are individuals with unique strengths and needs, we have noted some commonly encountered emotional potholes that challenge both beginning and experienced principals. The following scenarios emerge from our work. Each includes an illustration of the role of the coach in working through these issues. Each resonates with what Goleman calls the four components of EI: self-awareness, self-management, social awareness, and relationship management.

Making the Transition From "One of Us" to "One of Them." Most new principals have come up through the teaching ranks in their districts, if not at their own sites. Like it or not, in the culture of most schools, an administrator is no longer regarded by teachers as a colleague. A new principal may feel like the same person she was before donning the administrator hat, but she will be treated differently by friends, former colleagues, and community members. Recognizing and accepting change in how we are perceived can be a difficult adjustment.

> Within the first month of her first principalship, Susan was forced to respond to parent complaints about Jean, a friend and former teacher colleague. Jean expected unquestioning support from Susan; the parents were looking to their new principal to respond to their concerns. Susan was perplexed and torn by this situation, one that radically changed her relationship with a colleague of many years. Susan's coach helped her monitor her emotional responses to this situation, analyze Jean's interests and those of the students and parents, and develop an appropriate action plan. Susan's coach also helped her recognize the need to build a new support network where it was safe to share these difficult problems in confidence.

Becoming a Supervisor of Adults. Most new principals have little or no experience as supervisors and evaluators. It is a long emotional leap to become comfortable establishing clear expectations of staff and then following through on them. Tough personnel problems demand that principals manage their own emotions, including anger, empathy, and guilt; deal effectively with the emotional responses of adults; and use the system to serve the best interests of students.

> Mike did not expect to spend dozens of hours during his first months in the principalship dealing with the night custodian. But when rooms weren't being cleaned and the cafeteria wasn't set up for assemblies as requested, he knew he had to step in. His intervention was met with the night custodian's defensiveness and complaints about the lead custodian. Mike's initial reaction to this backlash was to back off for fear of hurting feelings and alarming the union and the district office. With his coach, Mike talked through his emotional reaction to this state of affairs—and as a result, he managed to build a process of accountability for the night custodian that involved the lead custodian, the district maintenance supervisor, and the classified employees union.

Living Under the Spotlight. Principals are surprised by the degree to which their every gesture is subjected to widespread scrutiny. The principalship is a form of celebrity (or notoriety) and requires some surrender of privacy and the freedom to be oneself. Principals must learn a new level of automatic metacognition and impulse control. Every vocalization, decision, and action must be filtered through the questions, *"How will this be interpreted? How will this serve my desired ends?"*

Jack was in a meeting with his coach when two parent volunteers entered his office asking for the key to a closet where supplies for the upcoming Halloween carnival were stored. His response to the two mothers was, "Please, I'm in a meeting. I can't lend you the key now, but I'll be out in a half an hour or so." It didn't take long for the word to get out among parent volunteers that Jack was rude and unappreciative. Jack's coach helped him to develop a less abrupt style of communication, to express appreciation, and to be more attuned to the ways in which people were likely to respond to him.

Letting Go of Emotional Responses to Problems. Principals are assaulted by dozens of problems large and small every day. In order to manage their personal stress, they must separate themselves from those problems. And in order to lead their sites effectively, they must set aside their gut responses to problems and approach them instead from a systems perspective.

Carlos was the first Latino principal of a school in transition from serving a largely African American student body to a student population that is primarily Asian and Latino. The previous administrator of the school was African American. It was not unusual for Carlos to be accused of racial bias in his handling of discipline incidents and personnel problems. In this charged environment, Carlos worked with his coach to set aside his anger at being called a racist. He learned to mediate his words and actions and to listen carefully to all parties. Perhaps most important, Carlos began to build inclusive systems and a culturally proficient staff at his site.

Letting Go of Perfectionism and Control. Most people achieve the principalship because they were very competent in their previous positions. They typically come from jobs that were much more contained, in which they could exercise direct, hands-on control. The principalship is more complex. It requires delegation along with acceptance of ambiguity and the lack of strict control. Living with this new tension can be very difficult for some novice administrators.

Elliott describes himself as "anal-retentive." In his first few months on the job, he panicked over all the things that were "not quite right" at his school. There were the staff members who showed up a little bit late, the messy classrooms, the teachers who were not teaching the adopted reading program, the nonexistent budget records, the poor cafeteria supervision . . . Elliott felt as if each of these issues and more were entirely his responsibility and considered himself obligated to make things right immediately. Because he lacked confidence in the ability of others to do things to his standards, he hesitated to delegate. Elliott's coach helped him to recognize that he could not turn his school around all at once or all by himself. Only by living with imperfection and sharing control could Elliott help his school truly progress. Once Elliott accepted these concepts, he was able to work with his coach to develop plans for delegation of tasks and for sharing leadership responsibilities.

Accepting That the Job Is Never Finished. Related to the need to let go of perfectionism and control is the requirement that administrators understand the principalship as a job with no boundaries—other than those set by the individual principals themselves.

Lucinda could not believe it. She had always worked very hard and never procrastinated. She had been on top of her work and consistently met her own high standards. But now she was in a daze, working from seven in the morning until nine at night on weekdays, and at least one day every weekend. She was held hostage by the paperwork to be reviewed, the meetings to be planned, the journals to be read. Lucinda worked with her coach to prioritize her work, to delegate tasks to others, and to manage her time. One afternoon, she and her coach did nothing but go through her in-box, deciding what could be ignored, what required a personal response, and what could be delegated. Finally, Lucinda articulated a set of promises to herself and to her family: she would be home for dinner four nights a week, and she would work no more than two weekend days each month.

Taking Care of Oneself. Most people who serve as principals are highly dedicated and very altruistic. They have a hard time recognizing, let alone taking care of, their own needs for support—whether those needs are clerical or emotional. To be effective, principals must learn that investing in their own well-being, including interests and relationships outside of school, is important to the well-being of their schools.

Julie was a mess. By her own accounts, she was working 70 hours a week. She was not eating regular meals, had stopped exercising, and was neglecting her husband and teenage daughter. Her coach helped her to recognize that the patterns she had slipped into were not sustainable and supported her to develop more effective management systems. Julie was able to give herself permission to block out quiet time to work at home to catch up on thinking and paperwork, as well as invest time and resources in her own professional development and physical and mental health.

Developing New Relationships With Authority. Many principals enter the job intimidated by superintendents, board members, and other administrators at higher levels. It is necessary for them to overcome this by learning to manage these relationships comfortably. They must also learn to manipulate the system in order to insure that personal and site needs are met. In addition, principals in many districts have to achieve an understanding about which of the overwhelming top-down mandates and expectations must be heeded, and which can be safely ignored.

One reason Roxanne was hired as principal was that she was a loyal and committed teacher. When the district told her of its plans to transfer two veteran teachers with histories of unsatisfactory performance to her site, she was torn between advocating for her site and being a "good soldier." She felt that the district was exploiting her, but she was afraid to assert herself. With her coach, Roxanne developed a strategy for dealing with the situation, and role-played the conversations she planned on having with the superintendent.

Balancing Relationships Against Productivity. Principals are often frustrated because they find they don't have enough time for people. In order to survive in their jobs, it is necessary for them to become more efficient in their relationships. They must learn to manage their conversations so they are short but still meet the emotional needs of the participants. There can be a painful tension between the desire to be relaxed and friendly and the need to be task-oriented.

Edward loved people—and was in danger of becoming the most popular but least effective principal in the history of Madrone School. Edward would listen to parents and teachers express their concerns for hours on end. He would chat about family and sports with custodians and trustees without regard to other demands on his time. He was building strong relationships, but he was not attending to other responsibilities; nor was he invested in a vision for his school. As Edward's coach shadowed him for a full day, Edward practiced keeping his conversations short, positive, and productive. He learned to use his daily calendar and tickler files as tools for following through on tasks. As Edward articulated his vision for his school, the strong relationships he had built with his staff served as a powerful base for school improvement.

Not Taking it Personally. Anyone who has been a school leader for any time at all will soon begin to speak of the need to acquire a "thick skin." Learning to manage emotional responses to criticism and conflict is essential to managing personal stress—and, as noted above, to being an effective problem-solver.

> José called his coach late on a Friday night. His supervisor had told him that the superintendent was receiving parent and teacher complaints about him. As a result, the superintendent would be conducting a survey and meeting with staff members to assess his performance. José felt attacked, angry, and devastated, all at the same time. But as he discussed this situation with his coach, he came to realize that all of this was a result of his willingness to take on the school's dysfunctional culture. If he mediated his emotions and worked *with* the superintendent, he could view this review process as an opportunity to expose the school's problems, consolidate his support, and build a mandate for change.

Each of the above issues draws upon professional knowledge and skills, but each also has emotional dimensions. An effective coach must be prepared to address both the cognitive and affective domains in helping a coachee through a variety of challenging situations.

There are a number of excellent sources of useful information for coaches in the area of emotional intelligence. First among them is *Primal Leadership,* by Goleman, Boyatzis, and McKee (2002). Additional resources are available on the Internet, including a simple self-assessment that can be taken by coaches and coachees on the Salum International Resources Web site (http://www.saluminternational.com/emotional_intelligence.htm).

ISSUES OF CULTURAL PROFICIENCY

In our diverse public schools, the emotional intelligence challenges of leadership are made even more complex by the particular demands of cross-cultural relationships.

Most educators have ample experience and are comfortable working with teachers and parents in the settings in which they have "grown up." But school leaders must learn to navigate the often-unforgiving and diverse cultural and emotional landscapes that exist both inside and outside of the education community. Encounters with new individuals, groups, and situations demand that principals be good listeners, keen observers of emotional response, and effective mediators of their own prejudices and personal communications.

Few jobs make as many demands upon an individual's ability to negotiate across cultures as the principalship. Here are a few examples of cross-cultural challenges we have encountered in our coaching practice:

- The Jewish administrator from the East Coast who had to overcome the suspicions of a large portion of the classified staff in a rural Western community that had little experience with his cultural group.
- A Latino principal who feared that any mistake he made would reflect not only on himself but also on his ethnic group.
- A white female principal who had to develop her own knowledge of and comfort with her school's Asian immigrant community.

Principals who are committed to working with their school communities often struggle with cultural and language barriers. These may exist between the principal and segments of the community, between staff and the community, within the community itself, or across all groups. We are often uncomfortable bringing these issues to the surface. We often make the false assumption that we all share the same cultural understandings and the same commitments around equity.

Lindsey, Robins, and Terrell (1999) outline five elements of cultural proficiency, calling upon school leaders to assess culture, manage the dynamics of difference, institutionalize cultural knowledge, and adapt to and value diversity. School leadership coaching often focuses on each of these elements. We believe that almost all school issues contain cross-cultural elements and suggest that there are both emotional intelligence and cross-cultural aspects to each of the scenarios we present in this book.

Leadership coaches need to be alert to issues of cultural proficiency and emotional intelligence and to have the courage to raise them. Leadership coaches create safe spaces in which to ask questions like "Could race have something to do with your reaction to this angry parent?" Leadership coaches understand that the exercise of the professional knowledge, skills, and abilities outlined by ISLLC is grounded in the inter- and intra-personal.

Reflection: Identify a cross-cultural challenge you have faced in your professional career. What did you learn by facing the challenge? What role did a mentor or other person play in helping you find your way through the situation?

THE CHALLENGE CONTINUES

The principalship seems to become more difficult every year. Many of those who were successful principals at one time—but who have moved on to become professors of educational administration or central office

Figure 2.1   Support for School Leaders

administrators—now question whether they could succeed as principals in today's climate. The complexities of the job, changing socioeconomic realities, ever-increasing expectations, and pressures resulting from the standards and accountability movements have all converged into a perfect storm that now threatens to batter principals and capsize their best efforts.

It is not only novice principals who are affected. Veterans also need the kind of support that leadership coaching provides. They find themselves in jobs that are very different from the ones they assumed even a few years ago. They must master new areas of knowledge and skills and contend with new challenges to their levels of emotional intelligence and cultural proficiency. In this regard, novice principals may, in fact, be better prepared than their more experienced colleagues to face change and to understand teaching and learning.

As our friend in Figure 2.1 illustrates, a school leader needs the support of both internal and external systems in order to keep standing. A leadership coach can be a critical component of an external support system, and a mentor can be an important internal support.

> *Reflection:* What might be other sources of internal and external support for school leaders?

School leadership is a great profession and life calling, if only because one can never master the job. There is always room for learning.

3

Building Relationships

I t is our opinion that despite different approaches and experience, all leadership coaches must bring certain foundational coaching skills to the table. These include *relationship building; listening, observing, and questioning;* and *giving feedback.*

Figure 3.1 Foundational Coaching Skills

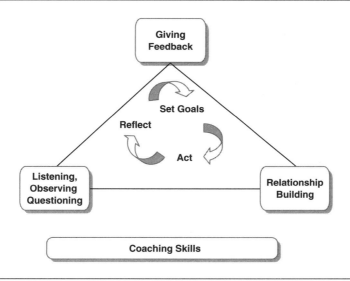

FOUNDATIONAL COACHING SKILLS

As represented in Figure 3.1, all coaching is centered on increasing the coachee's ability to *set goals* effectively, to *act* in pursuit of those goals, and to *reflect* upon those actions and their impacts. The coachee must be prepared to review and revise goals accordingly, setting new ones when appropriate. As a coach, you must be a skilled listener, observer, and questioner in order to help the coachee clarify context, goals, and impacts of actions taken. You must also cultivate the ability to provide useful feedback that will fuel the coachee's ongoing reflective practice. None of this is possible, however, unless you establish and maintain a relationship with your coachee that is characterized by trust and rapport.

RELATIONSHIP BUILDING

There are few places in life where we are more exposed than in positions of leadership. Our intelligence, our skill, our knowledge, our interpersonal relationships, even our physical appearance and fashion sense are subject to unceasing public scrutiny. Principals are all too familiar with this phenomenon. They are under tremendous pressure to please a number of diverse constituencies, and they are vulnerable on many fronts. They are also extremely busy. It may be a challenge, then, to lead principals to embrace a coaching relationship in which they are asked to slow down, take the time to reflect, and reveal their doubts and failures to a stranger.

In order to make coaching possible and to support a principal through the process, a coach must, at a minimum, have a trusting relationship with the coachee—one firmly grounded in the commitment to help the principal coachee achieve his or her goals.

> *The role of the coach is granted by the coachee based on trust. Without trust there can be no coaching. Trust will always be at stake during the process of coaching. Trust can increase and become more solid, and it can be taken away. It can be initially gained, then lost and afterwards recovered. Or it can be lost for good. The coach always moves along the thin cord of the coachee's trust. To take for granted the coachee's trust is one of the big mistakes a coach can make.*
>
> Rafael Echeverría and Julio Olalla,
> authors of *The Art of Ontological Coaching*

Building Trust

Job one for a coach is to build and maintain trust with the coachee. Powerful coaching simply cannot occur without it. As Echeverría and

Olalla make clear, trust is not static; it is established over time and it must be consciously and consistently nurtured.

Reflection: Think of someone other than a family member or personal friend in whom you have had a high degree of trust. List the characteristics of the individual that supported the establishment of trust.

Trust is an *assessment* that one individual makes about another. Like all assessments, its validity resides in the individual making the judgment. For example, I'm the one who decides whether or not to trust an auto mechanic. Is Joe at the Corner Auto Shop telling me the truth about what's wrong with my car? Is he honest in his billing? Does he know what he's doing? Will he have my car ready when he says he will? My level of trust may change based upon how I assess Joe's performance over time.

One way to think about trust is as an assessment of *sincerity, reliability,* and *competence.*

When we assess someone's *sincerity,* we are considering whether the individual's actions and internal conversations match their utterances. Do they mean what they say and say what they mean? Here are a few examples of what a coachee might be thinking when assessing a coach's sincerity:

"My coach says that he is completely here at my service, but I know he's busy. Does he mean it when he says he is available for me 24/7, or is he just being nice?"

"My coach tells me my problems aren't all that unusual, but she looks worried. Is she really thinking that I'm incompetent?"

"My coach sure seems like a 'good old boy.' Does he really care about the success of a woman like me?"

In essence, a coach must tell the truth in order to be assessed by the coachee as sincere. It is not necessary for the coach to verbalize every thought; but what the coach does say must be honest and truly reflect the coach's thoughts, feelings, and intentions. We determine if someone is sincere by matching what they say with their behaviors, including subtle body language, and word choices. A skilled coach is mindful of this and therefore always ensures in coaching conversations that words, body language, and actions are congruent.

Another factor in judging whether individuals are trustworthy is their *reliability.* Will they keep their commitments? As a coach, will you actually deliver what you promise? Will you follow through to meet the expectations you have established for yourself? As a coachee assesses a coach's reliability, thoughts such as these may come to mind:

> "My coach says he sometimes socializes with the superintendent, but he assures me that he will keep our coaching conversations confidential. I know he is sincere in his intentions, but can I rely on him to keep his mouth shut about our work together?"

> "She promised to help me plan next week's staff meeting. This is high stakes for me. Is she really going to call when she said she would?"

> "Last time we met, he promised to bring me some articles on block scheduling, but he didn't follow through. So much for him."

Finally, in order to be trusted, an individual must be assessed as *competent*. Coaches must provide evidence that they possess the knowledge and skills required to do the job. We all know people who are completely sincere and quite reliable but not particularly competent, and our trust in them is compromised as a result. A coachee might weigh these sorts of considerations in reflecting upon a coach's competence:

> "My coach has never worked in an urban school. Does he have any experience working with the sorts of issues I face here? Will he be able to help me?"

> "She has been away from site administration for six years. Can she help me with all of these new compliance issues?"

> "My supervisor tells me that I would have been inviting a union grievance if I had followed his advice. I'm not sure that he knows what he's talking about."

Coaches must be clear about the knowledge, skills, and experience they bring to the coaching relationship. They should also remember that their primary job is not to be a competent *principal*—that is the coachee's job—but rather a competent *coach*. It is frequently necessary for coaches to withhold their personal expertise so their coachees can develop individual, internal capacity.

It is important to remember that just as the coach must work to establish and maintain trust with the coachee, the principal must work to establish and maintain trust with the coach as well as with all of the various constituencies the principal serves. An effective coach supports the coachee in being perceived as sincere, reliable, and competent in the principalship.

Trust Building: Basic Steps

Here is a short checklist of the steps taken by effective coaches to build trusting relationships with their coachees:

- Demonstrate sincerity by

  - ✓ Being fully present in the coaching relationship
  - ✓ Demonstrating personal regard
  - ✓ Being truthful
  - ✓ Asking for permission
  - ✓ Admitting mistakes
  - ✓ Maintaining confidentiality

- Demonstrate reliability by

  - ✓ Clarifying expectations
  - ✓ Keeping commitments
  - ✓ Behaving consistently
  - ✓ Being available

- Demonstrate competence by

  - ✓ Letting your coachee know about your expertise and experience
  - ✓ Finding outside expertise in cases where you don't possess it
  - ✓ Remembering that your job is to be a competent coach, not a competent principal
  - ✓ Having high expectations of yourself and of the coaching relationship

A Caveat

Sometimes the fear of damaging the relationship or of undermining trust will cause a coach to hold back, to stop short of raising difficult questions or sharing challenging feedback. We remind you that serving as a leadership coach is a critical professional role requiring risk taking and clarity of purpose. It may seem paradoxical, but in our experience, bold coaches have the greatest impact and are most trusted by their coachees.

Building Rapport

> *Being in rapport is the ability to enter someone else's model of the world and let them know that we truly understand their model.*
>
> Michael Brooks, author of *Instant Rapport*

Trust is the ground upon which we build *rapport*, the safe and intimate place that allows for meaningful coaching. We define rapport as a state of harmony and understanding between two people. In a powerful coaching relationship, trust and rapport feed one another and create a space where tough issues can be addressed and where significant growth can occur.

Leadership coaches must consciously work to build rapport, especially in initial meetings with coachees.

As Sonia approached Blackwater Pond Elementary School, she reflected on her initial phone contact with David, her new coachee and the principal of this school. His voice sounded guarded as he talked about his school and his understanding of his involvement with a leadership coach. In spite of her best efforts on the phone, she sensed that he was hesitant about coaching.

Prior to their first meeting, Sonia found out a bit more about the school and David from her district office contact. She learned that he was the third principal in as many years. He had been a successful teacher and then assistant principal at Oliver Middle School for one year. David had been fast-tracked into the principalship, primarily because of a lack of experienced candidates for the position. Blackwater was portrayed as an underperforming school with a history of "problem" staff members.

Sonia knew that her first few moments with David would be important in establishing the coaching relationship. As David appeared in the reception area of the outer office, she stood up to greet him and extended her hand.

Rapport Building: Basic Steps

Many people who "hit it off" right away do so naturally and unconsciously. However, rapport can be built consciously by using deliberate verbal and nonverbal communication strategies. Because rapport building is essential to success in the private sector (no, that salesman may not really be all *that* interested in your kids), there has been a fair amount of research done in this area that can be applied to coaching school leaders. As you build a close relationship with your coachees, attend to the following steps.

Discover and share personal and professional connections. In American culture and in the busy world of school leadership, it is usually our impulse to get down to business and to do it right *now.* Some of us are hesitant to take the time to get to know our colleagues on a personal basis, to learn about their private lives and to find common friends, experiences, and interests. While coaching sessions should not be social time, we do encourage coaches to know and be known by their coachees on a personal level.

Be fully present in the conversation. As a coach, it is your responsibility to give your full attention to your coachee. You must tune out both internal and external distractions: the argument you had with your teenager that morning, the bad traffic on your way to your appointment, the smell of mildew emanating from the carpet in the principal's office—all of these must be shut out as you focus only on your coachee.

Be aware of your body language. Your eyes, face, posture, and gestures all communicate at least as much as your words. When we watch two individuals converse, we can see their rapport in the way they lean toward one another, in their eye contact, and in the dance of their gestures. In *Instant Rapport*, Michael Brooks (1989) suggests that rapport can actually be built by subtly mirroring an individual's gestures to establish a harmony that will extend into conversation and relationship.

Listen impeccably. We will talk more about listening in the next section, but here it must be said that active listening is critical to building rapport. The pioneering psychiatrist Karl Menninger is credited with pointing out, "Listening is a magnetic and strange thing, a creative force. The friends who listen to us are the ones we move toward. When we are listened to, it creates us, makes us unfold and expand."

Michael Brooks suggests we can build rapport by listening for and speaking to a person's way of processing information, which he claims falls into one of three categories: visual, auditory, and kinesthetic. When we build rapport through impeccable listening, we try to get ourselves into the skin of the other person and understand fully the way in which he or she is experiencing the world.

Communicate acceptance. It's impossible to feel rapport with someone whom you experience as even slightly threatening—or who conveys disdain, rejection, superiority, or contempt. Manifest acceptance is the foundation of rapport—and of all that is positive in relationships.

Sonia smiled at David and let him know she was pleased to meet him. She let him take the lead in the flow of the conversation, giving him her full attention as he showed her the way to his office. Once there, Sonia sat down, being careful to keep an open body position (arms relaxed and uncrossed, body directly facing the speaker). She remained focused on David and what he was saying. She listened intently to David as he described his school, nodding and using verbal responses such as "Uh hum . . . I see . . . Umm." She asked him a bit about his personal background and discovered a few things they had in common. They had attended the same MA program; they both had children; and both had taught middle school in the southern part of the state.

As the conversation proceeded, Sonia could see David relax and become more open and engaged in the discussion. He was less hesitant in his speech patterns and more animated as he described his family and past experiences. David looked directly at Sonia, smiled, and even laughed a few times as he described his feelings about his new assignment. At the end of their appointment, David asked, "So, when can you come back?"

As Sonia left David's office, she was confident that she had begun to establish rapport and trust, and she felt David was more open to having a coach. She had consciously done more listening than speaking. She had focused on attending to what he was saying and how he was saying it. At times she carefully used a few mirroring techniques and observed that he responded well to these. Sonia left the school looking forward to her work with David, satisfied that the time she had spent today building rapport with him would provide a solid foundation for coaching.

Exercise: The next time you are at a party or a mixer, approach a stranger and strike up a conversation. Make a conscious effort to establish rapport. Observe yourself and your partner throughout the conversation. What did you talk about? What did your body language communicate? What elements of your conversation contributed to your success or lack of success at establishing rapport?

4

Listening, Observing, and Questioning

Powerful coaching is grounded in the basic skills of listening, observing, and questioning. The coach is a different observer, able to help the coachee see new possibilities in an existing situation by providing new data and perspectives.

> *My coach has this uncanny ability to track what I am talking about on so many levels. I have come to notice that she is doing much more than just listening to what I am saying. She watches me carefully to see how I am feeling and what is going on below the surface. When we are in the middle of talking about some problem I am facing, she is able to hold my issue in the greater context of what she knows about me and where I have been and where I am going.*

Antonio, second-year principal at Chavez Middle School

Listening, observing, and questioning are complex, multidimensional processes. In even the simplest conversations, we attend to a speaker's words, vocal inflections, gestures, and facial expressions and to our own emotional reactions to the speaker. This broad spectrum of inputs makes up the gestalt of our listening.

By now, the notion of "active listening" is a cliché: Do you *hear* what we are saying? However, the fact that we *talk* about listening does not mean that we educators are good listeners. Nor are we particularly good observers. It is interesting to note that current efforts to drive school improvement by "data-based decision making" are all about improving our performance as observers and listeners.

We tend to think of communication as the act of transmitting and receiving information. This model may work between computers passing digital information back and forth without distorting or losing data. But humans are not hardwired, and all communication is filtered through our listening. It is shaped by our biases, experiences, intentions, and interpretations.

LISTENING TO WORDS

Listening includes attention to context and to nonverbal data. However, words alone convey huge amounts of information, information that is often underutilized. As you listen carefully to verbal communication, it is sometimes helpful to imagine you are reading a transcript rather than watching an individual speak. What are the facts and details embedded in the speaker's story? What do the speaker's word choices convey? Are the spoken messages free of generalizations? Free of bias? Of blame and finger pointing? Is the speaker reasoned in the choice of words used to describe the event or the person involved? Are there patterns of language or comments that tell us about the speaker's way of thinking?

Let's look at the comments of one new principal—we'll call her Joan—about some of her teachers:

> I think things are going well overall. I do have a bunch of older teachers who are constantly saying that things aren't fair. They want me to make the decisions but only the decisions they agree with and not the ones they do not agree with. They want me to be like the last principal—a bit top-down and directive.

Reflection: What do Joan's words tell you about her way of thinking and interacting?

There are only four sentences in Joan's statement. We have no nonverbal information and know nothing about the school except for what is conveyed in the statement. However, these four sentences hint at some significant issues that might emerge in working with this principal.

- Joan speaks in generalities ("things are going well," "a bunch," "constantly saying," "they want"). She seems to be making broad judgments. Is she backing up her opinions with data?
- Joan seems to have a dismissive attitude, referring to "older teachers" and "they" and to the former principal as "top-down."
- We can see the beginning of an unhealthy polarization here, an alienation between Joan and at least a portion of her staff.

Assertions and Assessments

Joan has constructed a story about her school, a story that is built upon a series of judgments. If Joan is like most people, she has confused her interpretations with reality. She will proceed to interact with her staff under the illusion that her story is *the* story. A powerful coach will help Joan recognize that her story is not reality. Rather, it is an interpretation; being open to other interpretations might open Joan to new and more productive ways of engaging with her staff.

In our coaching practice, we have found it helpful to be able to make the distinction between two types of speech known as *assertions* and *assessments*. The characteristics of these are derived from the work of linguist John Searle and philosopher Rafael Echeverría. They are among a group of contemporary thinkers who have taught us about the generative power of language.

We recognize that some readers may have trouble with this use of the words *assertion* and *assessment*. Assessment, in particular, carries a particular meaning for most educators in regard to its application to testing. For the purpose of our discussion, we ask you to suspend any preconceived definitions of these terms and entertain the ones we introduce here.

Searle maintains that assertions and assessments are two of the small number of basic speech acts that can be found in all language in all cultures. Assertions describe facts that can be corroborated by a witness. Here are some examples:

"It is 73° F in this room."

"Susana scored 1500 points on the SAT."

"Four parents attended the last site council meeting."

"Three students did not complete the assignment."

Each of these statements is either true or false, measured by some kind of commonly held standard (such as degrees Fahrenheit). They reside outside of the speaker in the sense that they do not represent the speaker's opinion or judgment. Instead, they are attempts to describe an objective reality.

Contrast the above assertions with these assessments:

"It is hot in this room."

"Susana is smart."

"Parents here just don't want to get involved."

"John has low expectations of his students."

Assessments are not true or false by any objective measure. Rather, they are judgments or opinions. They reside in the speaker. For example, when I say, "It is hot in this room," I am commenting on my internal experience. Assessments are speech acts that change our experience of reality and shape our future actions. They impact the way in which we behave. They are the fabric from which our interpretations are constructed.

There is nothing wrong with making assessments. In fact, we have to make them in order to function effectively in the world. However, we get in trouble when we confuse our assessments, or interpretations, with assertions, or facts. Strong assessments are well grounded in assertions; weak assessments are often pulled out of thin air. Joan, for example, has confused her assessments with assertions. Many people do. She has made a string of assessments that will shape her actions and determine the ways in which others will react to her. When she states, "I do have a bunch of older teachers who are constantly saying that things aren't fair," she paints the picture of a crew of cranky veterans who are going to get in her way. Her language includes a number of assessments ("bunch," "older," "constantly") and no clear assertions. An effective coach might help Joan to unpack her statement and arrive at new interpretations.

COACH: "Joan, who are these teachers, and what is their complaint?"

JOAN: "Sandy, a teacher who has been here for a long time, told me that she and a couple of the other veteran teachers are not happy because we are changing reading programs. She says they invested a lot of time in developing their literature-based program, and they don't want to give it up."

COACH: "So we are talking about a small group of teachers who are hesitant to give up a program that they have made a personal investment in. Have you thought about ways in which you can harness their experience with and interest in literature-based programs to help you to move them toward your literacy initiative?"

In addition to our assessments of other people and external experiences, the assessments we make about ourselves can have a huge impact on our effectiveness. In the Resource section at the end of this book, we offer a worksheet that will guide you or a coachee through a reflection on self-assessment (see Resource A).

Separating Assertions from Assessments: Basic Steps

Coaches can guide their coachees to an awareness of assessments and assertions by:

- Listening for situations in which the coachee is confusing assessments with assertions.
- Helping the coachee ground and reevaluate assessments by asking three questions:
  - ✓ Assessment for the sake of what?
  - ✓ Assessment against what standards?
  - ✓ Assessment based on what assertions?

- Pointing out self-assessments the coachee may make that are not well grounded and therefore are likely to limit possibilities.

NONVERBAL COMMUNICATION

Albert Mehrabian (1972) has conducted research demonstrating that only about 7 percent of the emotional meaning of a message is communicated through the exchange of words. Some 38 percent is communicated by vocal intonation, and the remaining 55 percent is expressed through gestures, posture, facial expressions, and other physical cues.

In this era of the Internet, e-mail, and videoconferencing, we still spend huge amounts of money bringing people together in the same physical space. We may accomplish a lot in our abstract, digital worlds, but we remain (thank goodness!) animals that rely on proximity, on sight, smell, touch, and a wealth of other subtle cues essential to communication.

The ability to interpret nonverbal cues is the hallmark of a truly skilled listener. Paying attention to how a message is communicated is often more telling and informative than the actual content of the message. When attending to nonverbal communication, the listener watches facial expressions and body language for clues about the internal state of the speaker. Listening for the speaker's vocal inflections (monotone, tense, excited) and the rate of speech (rapid, calm, agitated, hesitant) provides additional clues. What is the body position of the speaker? Closed? Relaxed? Fidgeting?

Let's visit a few principals and "listen" to what they might be communicating to their coaches.

As Maria walks out to meet her coach on Monday morning, she is moving slowly and sighs to herself as she enters the outer office. Although she says, "I am glad to see you," her voice is slow and heavy. Her coach wonders what has affected Maria's mood. She knows that one of her goals in today's session will be to understand Maria's affect.

Lance is very quiet in this initial meeting. He is not forthcoming in responding to his coach's questions, often answering in just a few words. Although cordial, he sits with his arms crossed in front of his chest and does not make consistent eye contact. The coach predicts that she is going to have to do some groundwork to win Lance's trust and buy-in to the coaching process.

John is friendly and outgoing and typically uses humor during his meetings with his coach. He is relaxed and frequently shares personal stories about his family. When his coach asks him a question about difficult school issues, he usually reflects and takes his time responding. He often expresses his appreciation for the opportunity to confide in a "safe" person. But today he is short-tempered. He interrupts the coach and has gotten up and left the office three different times to give his secretary tasks. He is playing with a pen on his desk and seems not to be focusing on the topic at hand.

As Tony observes the staff meeting at his coachee Richard's school, he is pleased at the outset to see that Richard has taken him up on his suggestion to have teachers present some key agenda items as a means to develop and strengthen shared leadership. Then Tony begins to notice that Richard is having a hard time keeping his feelings to himself about what is being shared by teachers. He frowns and moves around in his seat in an agitated manner. He is also taking notes and making comments to the assistant principal seated at his side.

In each of these cases, nonverbal messages may be much more important than the coachees' utterances.

Exercise: Flip on the TV and watch an interview show with the sound off. How much information can you gather just by watching gestures and facial expressions?

Observing Emotion and Mood

Our work would be easy if it only required us to master organizational, operational, and pedagogical matters. But because the business of coaching school leaders happens in a human context, we must be prepared to observe and address affective issues, the domains of mood and emotion.

While emotion and mood are closely related, there is a distinction between the two concepts. Emotions are immediate and are often triggered by events. They can be hard for us to control. Goleman (1998; Goleman et al.,

2002) reminds us that effective leaders mediate their emotional reactions and are highly conscious of the impact their emotional states have on others.

Mood is related to emotion, but is a more enduring sensibility. Because mood is a deeper and more durable state, it has a huge impact upon an individual or organization's efficacy. Think about the differences in mood between a staff meeting at a school that is coming together around common goals and one at a school that is mired in resistance to change. Mood is a predisposition to emotion and action.

Individuals operate in moods that leave them inclined to react in particular ways. A principal who is in a depressed and discouraged mood—such as Maria, in the example above—may be less than enthusiastic when, for instance, a special needs student steps in the door to register for school. If such a mood persists, it will pervade the school and significantly harm the culture there. Leaders help to shape the moods of their organizations.

Because moods and emotion exist in individuals and in organizations, effective coaches are alert to the emotional state of both the coachee and the coachee's school. These coaches observe the principal's emotions and mood, monitor the emotions and mood at the school, and are prepared to intervene in both if need be.

Leadership coaches would be well advised to read *Emotions Revealed,* in which author Paul Ekman (2003) provides a short course in observing, understanding, and intervening in human emotion. Ekman has made a career of cataloguing universal human emotions and the facial expressions accompanying them. He offers the opportunity to learn what for most of us is only intuitive: the skill of observing the emotional states of others.

Emotion is very much grist for the mill of coaching. Powerful coaches observe the emotional states of their coachees and how those emotions are experienced by others. A coach's own emotional reaction to a coachee is valuable data in the coaching process. In doing so, they take advantage of what psychoanalysts call *countertransference,* the coach's own emotional involvement in the interaction with the coachee as a source of insight.

GATHERING DATA, OBSERVING THE CONTEXT

While we have focused primarily on how coaches listen to and observe their coachees, it is important to note that leadership coaches cannot rely upon one-on-one conversations with coachees as their only source of data. Remember that the power of coaching lies in our ability to be different observers and help our coachees develop new interpretations and possibilities. We must apply our listening and observing skills to other sources of information, including

- 360° survey instruments (a sample is included in Resource C) that solicit feedback from a coachee's supervisors, subordinates, peers, and community;

- situations in which coachees are doing "real work," such as facilitating staff meetings, conferencing with parents, and supervising teachers;
- evidence of school effectiveness, including test data, classroom observations, and surveys; and
- coachee logs, reflections, and diaries.

RECURSIVE LISTENING

Recursive listening is defined as the act of *listening to listening.* There is a metacognitive dimension to effective listening and observing. Coaching requires the ability to focus completely upon the coachee and his or her environment. As coaches, we must be fully present as listeners and observers.

Coaches as good listeners learn to shut down the inner voice that is framing a response instead of attending to a speaker. They cultivate the ability to ignore their own grumbling stomachs and quiet their internal distracters ("I need to remember to call the office after this appointment"). Even as we shut down irrelevant internal noise, we can learn a great deal about our coachees and ourselves by *listening to our listening.*

In the kind of simple one-on-one coaching interaction illustrated in Figure 4.1, the coach must ask

- What do I hear and observe from the coachee (A)?
- How is the coachee listening and observing me (B)?
- What can I learn from observing my own listening (C)?

In other words, in a coaching conversation, the coach clearly can learn a lot by attending to the coachee's communication. The coach can also learn something about the coachee's disposition and skills by observing the ways in which the coachee listens to her. In listening to our own listening, we ask ourselves these sorts of questions:

- What is my emotional reaction to this coachee? (This is the sort of data called *countertransference* by psychoanalysts, who recognize its clinical importance.) Does she make me like her and want to engage with her? If I am reacting in this way to her, how might others react?

Figure 4.1   Reciprocal Listening

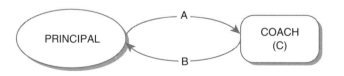

Figure 4.2   Multilevel Listening

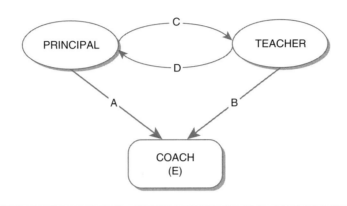

- Which of my negative and positive biases and "hot buttons" does this coachee trigger?
- As I observe myself in this conversation, what does my deep intuition tell me might be going on here?

Taking the notion of recursive listening just a bit further, Figure 4.2 illustrates the kind of complex listening that might take place as a coach observes a conversation between a teacher and a principal.

In this example, the coach's listening and observing skills must extend through five dimensions:

1. What do I hear and observe from the principal (A)?

2. What do I hear and observe from the teacher (B)?

3. What is the principal hearing and observing from the teacher (C)?

4. What is the teacher hearing and observing from the principal (D)?

5. What can I learn from observing my own listening (E)?

QUESTIONING

In the coaching relationship, questioning can serve both to inform the coach and to influence the coachee. In the first case, questioning is one of the ways in which a coach gathers information that will help to assess a coachee's needs and context. In the second, questioning is a powerful tool for helping a coachee clarify his own thinking, develop new interpretations, and discover new possibilities.

Regardless of their specific purpose, effective questions generally share some common characteristics, examples of which are included in Table 4.1.

Table 4.1   Six Characteristics of Effective Questions

Effective questions are	They sound like this:	Not like this:
Open ended	Tell me about your teaching experience. What do you think about . . .?	Where did you teach? Do you believe in . . .?
Invitational	It would be great to hear about . . . Would you consider . . .?	Why on earth would you . . .? Why don't you . . .?
Specific	How often does she . . .? What does it look like when . . .?	Does she . . . much? What will happen if . . .?
Evocative	What might this mean? Let's speculate about . . .	What does this mean? What will happen if . . .?
Positively or neutrally biased	What might you learn from this? Tell me what you were thinking.	What's up with . . .? What did you think would happen?
Challenge assessments	What evidence do you have that . . .? How could that be interpreted differently?	What is wrong with . . .? What's your feeling about . . .?

Exercise: This exercise is to be conducted with a close friend *only.* Ask the question, "Do you love me?" ten different ways, conveying ten different meanings. Use only these four words. You can do it. We know you can!

As this exercise will illustrate, effective questions are constructed of words, certainly, but also of nonverbal cues. Remember that questions do more than issue a request for a response; they communicate a great deal about the questioner. Effective questioning is inextricably linked to effective listening, and because of this it is key to the relationship between coach and coachee.

We will return to this topic in Chapter 7, where we will explore mediational questioning, a form of questioning that helps the coachee shift his or her ways of doing and being.

Figure 4.3   What Do YOU See?

BIAS IN LISTENING, OBSERVING, AND QUESTIONING

What do you see in Figure 4.3?

Most people who have grown up in developed countries see two people, perhaps an adult and a child, standing outside or inside a building. Individuals who live all of their lives in the African bush are likely to see a mother with a package on her head, standing with a child under a tree.

This illustrates the reality that each of us brings a unique set of biases to our observations, and every coach brings personal points of view to the coaching role. This is not necessarily a negative phenomenon, but it is something that we must keep in mind as coaches. Our gender, culture, age, and experiences all shape the ways in which we perceive our coachees and their contexts. These attributes also influence the ways in which we are perceived by them.

A coach who has spent most of her career in elementary schools will see high schools from a different perspective than an individual who has done most of her work at the secondary level. A Latino coach may bring a different perspective to issues of student discipline than an African American coach. A male coach may be received differently by a female coachee than a female coach would be.

We claim that one of the fundamental strengths a coach brings to the coaching relationship is the fact that he or she is a different observer, with a different perspective. The biases brought by individual coaches to their listening, observing, and questioning can be a source of power and richness in coaching—as long as the coach is aware of the ways in which they are manifest and is open in sharing those biases with the coachee.

In Resource A, we have included a worksheet designed to help coaches think about the inherent biases they bring to their coaching relationships.

5

Providing Feedback

T he third basic skill a coach must have is the ability to provide useful feedback to a coachee, feedback that will fuel ongoing reflective practice.

> *Effective feedback gives an individual or group clear, concise verbal and/or written data about events, patterns or conditions of behavior or organizational culture for the purpose of improved performance. Providing feedback is a process which includes observing an action or system and gathering information about it for the purpose of evaluation or corrections.*
>
> Patricia McLagan and Peter Krembs, authors of *On the Level: Performance Communication That Works*

As a different observer, the coach is able to see what the coachee cannot. Coaches often share observations by providing direct feedback. Just when and how we provide this feedback depends upon the coachee's readiness to hear what we have to say. It hinges on both our relationship with our coachee and the coachee's capacity to receive and apply the feedback.

Anyone who has been coached in a sport knows the power of an observant coach. The golf pro who suggests a slightly different grip, the swimming coach who points out a too-frequent breathing pattern—both draw your attention to subtle behaviors that are invisible to you but if changed can significantly improve your performance.

School leaders receive feedback regularly, but it is almost always indirect and informal. It accompanies everyday interactions, events, and accomplishments. Strong leaders are attuned to this informal feedback and use it to shape their practice. Unfortunately, formal feedback systems are very weak in most school settings. Most principal supervision systems consist of one or two meetings a year and an annual summative report. Many supervisors lack the time to provide principals with meaningful formative feedback. In addition, feedback from a supervisor, however accurate, is colored by the supervisor's authority.

Feedback from a coach is different because a coach has no formal power in relation to the coachee. The feedback a coach shares with a coachee is confidential and poses no threat to job security. It is safe, it serves the coachee's best interests, and it is all about improving practice. A coachee can challenge a coach's feedback and remain confident that an issue raised by a coach will not wind up on a year-end evaluation.

> *Reflection:* Think of a time when someone gave you feedback that helped you to be better at something. What were the characteristics of the feedback and the way in which it was delivered that made it effective?

FEEDBACK: BASIC STEPS

Here are some simple guidelines for providing feedback in the coaching process:

The coachee should share in determining the goal, type, and purpose of the feedback. One of the most effective paths in sharing feedback is through the door marked "Open here." When a coachee asks you to share your observations, it is an invitation to powerful coaching as well as an indication that the coachee is a committed learner.

> *You know, I sometimes don't listen when I am impatient and I have been working on that. I tune out or fiddle with things on my desk. If you notice that happening when you are with me, would you give me some feedback on that?*

At times you may find that you need to seek permission to share your feedback with a coachee. Assuming you have a trusting relationship with your coachee, be bold in offering feedback.

> *Would you mind if I shared a few observations about the conversation I just observed between you and your secretary? I noticed some things that may be contributing to that tension you were mentioning the last time I was here.*

Here you have asked permission and linked the permission to your purpose in providing the feedback. By providing feedback to address an expressed need, you are laying the foundation for providing more personal feedback at a later date as the need arises.

Provide feedback that is aligned with coachee and school needs. Just as a swim coach is standing alongside the pool, stopwatch in hand, looking for the change in breathing patterns that could improve a swimmer's time, a leadership coach is constantly scanning for data that could provide the coachee with feedback of strategic importance.

For example, you have noted that your coachee principal complains repeatedly of being overwhelmed. You have observed that she hesitates to delegate basic clerical tasks to her office staff and does not share leadership effectively with her assistant principal or teachers. As you begin to help her develop a process for writing this year's school plan, you realize that this conversation will also allow you to provide her with feedback about her hesitancy to delegate and to offer instruction to help her delegate the tasks necessary to complete the school planning process.

> *You know, there is something I have noticed this year which I would like to share with you. My observations are about how you appear to delegate tasks and share responsibilities. Since we are talking about how to make the planning process successful, this might be a good time to share some observations and ideas with you. What do you say?*

Effective feedback is grounded in data. The coach's goal is to provide the coachee with assertions (data) that will lead the coachee to make an assessment that in turn will lead to a change in behavior. The more concrete and specific the data, the easier it will be for your coachee to see and hear what the data suggest. Assessments in and of themselves—"You don't do a very good job of delegating"—don't make for effective feedback. Assertions do.

COACH: "I've noticed you are doing a number of tasks that other principals delegate. For example, you are keeping the school's books and facilitating all of the grade level meetings."

PRINCIPAL: "Everybody else is so busy, I feel like I have to take those things on."

COACH: "Now you are talking about a school planning process in which you will be doing the writing on your own. What might be some of the consequences of that approach?"

PRINCIPAL: "Aside from grinding myself into the ground? I suppose there might be less buy-in."

COACH: "Possibly. I have observed that you really hesitate to share responsibilities. I'd like to explore your reasons for this pattern and help you to set up some mechanisms that will make it easier for you to delegate. A good vehicle for this might be around the school plan since you already understand the limitations of doing it alone."

As you look to provide feedback, remember that your data must be objective and your assessments firmly grounded in assertions. Your work as a coach requires you to be a neutral observer of the coachee and the events surrounding the coachee. A statement such as "You are allowing a few people to dominate your staff meeting" is not likely to be as well received as "During your meeting, I heard four of the twenty-two teachers speak, two of them three times each. It appeared that you made a decision based on those four voices. How do you think the rest of the staff interpreted this exchange?"

Provide feedback comparing planned outcomes to actual outcomes. Because school leadership coaching is an ongoing process, it allows us to meet with coachees to discuss their planning for activities or events, to observe them, and to debrief with them afterwards. During the initial planning stage, a coach can help a coachee clarify goals as well as identify the kinds of feedback the coachee would like to receive.

COACH: "So, we are going to be observing Mike in the classroom today, and I am also going to observe your post-observation conference. Could you share what you hope to accomplish with Mike through this process?"

PRINCIPAL: "Mike and I have been talking about the number of kids who are failing his algebra class. I want to bring him around to recognizing the need to do more direct instruction and to provide more individualized help to some of his students."

COACH: "What would you like me to watch for in the post-observation conference?"

PRINCIPAL: "I want to get Mike to see that he has to change what he is doing. In the past when I have conferenced with him and pointed out these sorts of problems, he has become very defensive. Those conferences never went anywhere."

Link outcomes to leadership behaviors. Feedback that is framed as "when you did X, it produced Y" is very persuasive.

PRINCIPAL: "Mike seemed OK with the observation. I'm surprised he didn't realize that group of kids was off task."

COACH: "You helped him to see what is going on in the class, and he did not respond defensively. When you showed him the data you had collected on student engagement and completion of the work, he came to his own conclusions."

Feedback is more likely to be received positively when it is delivered through acknowledgment of a coachee's areas of strength. Coachees look to their coaches for reassurance and support. They are more open to growth when feedback is not perceived as a challenge to their competence.

COACH: "You collected data in Mike's class that clearly illustrated the experience of the at-risk kids in there. You presented him with lots of strategies he could use with the class."

PRINCIPAL: "Then why was it so hard for me to get him to commit to any next steps?"

COACH: "Is it possible that because you had collected and shared so much observation data, and have so much expertise around teaching strategies, that he felt overwhelmed? You could be a tremendous resource to Mike, but you are having a hard time getting through to him. Is it possible that he is feeling intimidated by you?"

Pay attention to timing. Feedback needs to be given when it is likely to be received. Poorly timed feedback may fall on deaf ears or may erode the trusting relationship the coach has worked so hard to build. There may be times when the coach observes a behavior that is working against the coachee but decides to hold off on sharing this observation. Powerful coaching occurs over time, and it may be weeks or months before the right opportunity arises to present sensitive feedback. The deeper the relationship between coach and coachee, the stronger the trust and the bolder the coach can be. Feedback and relationship are mutually reinforcing factors. Bold and appropriate feedback properly delivered builds the coaching relationship, and this allows for the continued sharing of effective feedback.

Positive feedback is important. Feedback has the potential to inspire our coachees. Look for opportunities to recognize their effective practices and strengths. School leadership is a tough and lonely business, and coachees often need the reinforcement that coaches can provide through positive feedback. Keep the feedback grounded in solid evidence. Global praise will do little to inspire and support. It is much like fast food—satisfying for a short time but with little nutritional value for the long haul.

BUILDING REFLECTIVE PRACTICE

As we illustrated in Figure 3.1, the coaching process is organized around a cycle of reflective practice, a cycle which continuously flows from goal setting to action to reflection. The goal of the coaching process is to develop self-actualized leaders who are always engaged in this cycle. Coaches support the development of reflective practice through relationship, listening, observing, questioning, and by providing feedback.

In Part II of this book, we will explore the deeper strategies that a leadership coach can bring to the coaching relationship, and we will apply these strategies to real issues we have confronted in our coaching practice.

PART II

Blended Coaching Strategies

In Part I of this book, we shared our general definition of coaching and outlined our case for coaching as an essential tool for the professional development of school leaders. We also reviewed the basic skills that effective coaches bring to their practice.

In Part II we explore the fundamental structure of coaching conversations and relationships—what we call coaching strategies. We suggest that effective leadership coaches draw upon a variety of coaching strategies and move fluidly between them through a process we call Blended Coaching Strategies. We suggest that there are two basic approaches to coaching, instructional coaching and facilitative coaching. Within and between those broad categories, we discuss consultative, collaborative, and transformational approaches. Finally, we suggest that the goal of school leadership coaching has to be systems change that has a lasting and positive impact upon students.

6

What Is Blended Coaching?

Though this be madness, yet there is method in 't.

William Shakespeare

I have yet to see any problem, however complicated, which, when you looked at it in the right way, did not become still more complicated.

Poul Anderson

There's more than one way to skin a cat.

Folk wisdom

Coaching is a complex art, and we are convinced there is no single "right" way to approach it. Certainly we do not own any unique or exclusive set of ideas around coaching. We have identified the basic skills we believe to be essential to successful leadership coaching: relationship building; listening, observing, and questioning; and giving feedback. Effective coaches use a variety of strategies as they apply these generic skills. They draw upon a number of coaching approaches, moving quickly and flexibly through them as required during the course of their coaching sessions.

We have developed a *Blended Coaching Strategies* model as a way to describe the practice of these powerful leadership coaches. We arrived at this design through a variety of experiences, including many years of coaching teachers and principals as well as training in cognitive coaching, ontological coaching, life coaching, and peer coaching. Because leadership coaching is a relatively new approach, research about it is ongoing. Our own research and that of related fields, however, appear to validate Blended Coaching Strategies as a way of thinking about the coaching process.

If we have made a unique contribution to the community of coaching practice, it is in acknowledging that effective coaches apply and meld a variety of strategies. We suggest that all coaching can be discussed within the context of Blended Coaching Strategies and that this framework is helpful in planning, implementing, and evaluating leadership coaching.

As prospective coaches work to master the strategies we introduce here, they might also choose to study and practice other approaches. We hope the literature included in the References section of this book will provide a springboard for readers into the many other available sources of useful information about leadership coaching strategies.

WAYS OF DOING, WAYS OF BEING

Most of the complex learning in which we humans engage involves changing both how we do things (our external behaviors) and who we are (our internal selves). Think about the process of learning to drive. Initially, you learned *how* to steer, to accelerate, to apply the brakes, to look to the right and the left before making a turn. You were nervous when you took even a short drive in your own neighborhood. Over time and with practice, however, the behaviors essential to driving successfully became almost automatic. You internalized them, found yourself comfortable with the process, and *became* a driver.

Jack wants to build a strong team with his two assistant principals at Highline High. He says he is committed to sharing leadership with them and to building their capacity as future principals. For the first time in his career as a principal, he is meeting weekly with his APs to talk about "big picture" issues. Working in concert with them, he has organized a plan for rotating responsibilities that will allow each AP to take on new and expanded instructional leadership roles. In addition, Jack is examining his own habits of holding power and problems close to his vest and expecting his APs to somehow magically anticipate and unquestioningly comply with his vision and desires.

In order to build a capable leadership team at his site, Jack is changing both *what he does* (by building new structures for communication and shared leadership) and *who he is* (by learning to relax his need for command and control).

Coaches must be prepared to support their coachees in learning to do new things—and old things in new ways. They must also be prepared to support their coachees in learning new ways of being—and changing old ways of being. These two dimensions of growth are closely linked. When we change what we do, we change who we are, and vice versa. A particular coaching interaction may center on either side of this dynamic, and this will influence the coach's choice of strategy.

School leaders need assistance to develop both their ways of doing and their ways of being. Learning on one side of the equation will impact the other. For example, it would not be unusual for a coach to assist a novice principal to prepare for a parent advisory meeting by helping the principal clarify the goals for the meeting, develop an agenda, and review mechanisms for increasing attendance. The coach is helping the principal with managerial steps, the things a principal *does*, that are prerequisite to involving parents in decision making. The coach might then attend and observe the meeting, watching for the ways in which the principal communicates with parents and responds to concerns and suggestions. In sharing feedback with the principal, the coach offers the opportunity to reflect upon the principal's interactions and to learn new ways of being with parents.

Table 6.1 offers a few examples of related *ways of doing* and *ways of being*.

Because a coach must be able to help the coachee learn both new ways of doing and new ways of being, we suggest coaches be prepared to apply two fundamental strategies: *instructional coaching* and *facilitative coaching*.

Table 6.1   Examples of *Doing* and *Being*

Ways of Doing	*Ways of Being*
Planning an agenda for a parent advisory meeting.	Embracing and utilizing parent involvement and voice.
Building a weekly time schedule to maximize classroom observation time.	Examining all decisions through the lens of impact upon instruction.
Providing teachers with student achievement data.	Building and facilitating a learning community focused on student achievement.
Meeting timelines and following procedures in evaluating staff.	Using the supervision process to uphold high standards and to support ongoing professional growth.

INSTRUCTIONAL COACHING
AND FACILITATIVE COACHING

Sometimes it is appropriate for a coach to teach, to use didactic methods in order to help a coachee to achieve a goal. Coaches typically use *instructional* strategies when they are focusing on a coachee's *way of doing.* For example, to help a coachee get into classrooms more often, a coach might provide an article on time management and work with the coachee to set up new office systems. The coach might shadow the coachee and suggest concrete changes in behavior and process that would make it possible for the coachee to protect the time set aside for classroom observations. Each of these instructional steps would help the principal do a better job of getting into classrooms.

Over time, we change who we are by changing what we do. However, instructional strategies have limitations. They may encourage dependence rather than independence. They teach specific knowledge and skills but fall short when it comes to building fundamental capacity. Coaches can help coachees internalize learning and be transformed by it through *facilitative* strategies, strategies that are constructivist in nature. These support the coachee in learning new *ways of being* through observation, reflection, analysis, reinterpretation, and experimentation.

Let's examine the distinction between these two fundamental coaching strategies as they might apply to Jack, the principal in our earlier example who is committed to building a strong leadership team at Highline High. We will assume that Jack has approached his coach for assistance. Jack's coach might use instructional strategies to help him set up management and governance structures. The coach might share his own experience, provide informative articles, and arrange visits with Jack to other high school sites. To help Jack learn to empower others, however, his coach would take a facilitative approach. This might include observing Jack as he interacts with his assistant principals and providing feedback, asking Jack to reflect on his observed behavior relative to his goals. Jack's coach might ask him to examine his deep assumptions about power, control, and responsibility. His coach might also ask him to role-play conversations with the APs, to try out new ways of operating, and then to step back and evaluate them.

THE MÖBIUS STRIP

Effective coaches move between instructional and facilitative domains as they strive to address coachee needs and accelerate coachee effectiveness. We represent the fluidity of this process by portraying it in the form of a Möbius strip. As we illustrate in Figure 6.1, Blended Coaching Strategies do not occur along a continuum but rather in a dynamic process.

To make a Möbius strip, bring the two ends of a piece of paper measuring about 1 inch by 8 inches together to form a circle. Twist one end

Figure 6.1   Blended Coaching Strategies as Möbius Strip

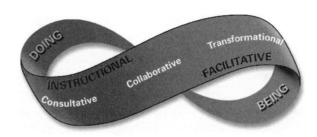

180° and tape it to the other. Now use a pen or a pencil to trace a line down the middle of the strip. You will find that the line is continuous; you have created a one-sided three-dimensional object. To deepen the mystery, use scissors to split the strip by cutting along the line you have drawn.

The Möbius strip represents a coaching process that is fluid, one in which ways of doing and ways of being are inextricably linked together as well as to the instructional and facilitative strategies that support them.

SOME CAVEATS

Most coaches find Blended Coaching Strategies to be a comfortable and rational way of envisioning the coaching process. But mastering this approach demands discipline and practice, as coaches must learn to move effectively between facilitative and instructional strategies.

Many educators have been trained in *cognitive coaching*, which provides participants with a strong set of facilitative skills. Cognitive coaching makes a clear distinction between the coaching role and the roles of consultant and collaborator. This model suggests that each of these roles has its place, but each function is distinct, with the cognitive coaching role as default. In our experience, leadership coaches trained in cognitive coaching often have very strong facilitative coaching skills, but struggle with a tension between the vision of coaching they have been taught— "Cognitive Coaching is a non-judgmental process of mediation" (Costa & Garmston, 2002, p. 29)—and their recognition of the need to use instructional strategies in the coaching process. Cognitive coaching acknowledges the consultative and collaborative functions but suggests that "each function plays a significantly different role, with very different mechanisms and intentions" (Costa & Garmston, 2002, p. 9). We have found that in the high-stakes environment of school administration, coaches need to be able to fluidly draw upon a broad repertoire of strategies, including instructional strategies, in the course of any coaching conversation. Thus, our model builds upon the outstanding work of Costa and Garmston and others in articulating a constructivist approach to coaching, while integrating other more didactic strategies.

Figure 6.2   The Blended Coaching Dance

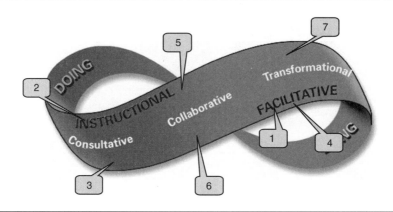

Some coachees do not possess the internal capacity to develop new knowledge and understandings through facilitative coaching. In these cases, it is simply more efficient and effective to share information, advice, and opinions using an instructional approach. But this should not be taken to mean we advocate coaching as "telling." Sitting down with a coachee and sharing war stories—"this is what happened to me . . . this is what I did. . . . this is what you should do . . ."—is decidedly *not* a coaching strategy we endorse.

Our experience and research both suggest that a blended approach to coaching is most effective for school leaders. Facilitative strategies have the potential to produce powerful personal growth, and instructional strategies support the development of the knowledge and skills required for success on the job. Leadership coaches must cultivate the ability to recognize, on the spot, which approach is likely to be most effective, and to move easily from one to the other as the situation demands.

In Figure 6.2, we highlight a sequence of selected coaching interventions as Mara supports John, a high school principal, in leading improvements in algebra instruction at Ringwood, a large comprehensive high school.

1. Using *facilitative* methods, Mara helps John to clarify his concerns and goals in relation to algebra instruction. She also uses facilitative coaching to help him identify teacher leaders and the communication processes he'll use to involve the faculty and parent community.

2. In *instructional* mode, Mara identifies a number of potential sources of student data that should be useful to John, and shows him how to interpret the data. She also provides John with templates of department meeting agendas that other schools use to plan and monitor program improvements.

3. In the *instructional consultative* role, Mara researches potential model programs for Ringwood, recommends that he visit a school with a model program, and recommends employing a consultant to assist the math department leadership team.

4. In the *facilitative* role, Mara leads John through the process of identifying potential barriers to the implementation of an improvement plan.

5. John and Mara visit math classrooms at Ringwood, and Mara uses *facilitative* questioning to help John to ground his assessments of the instructional practices observed and to outline next steps. She uses *instructional* coaching as she shares ideas for schoolwide professional development strategies with John.

6. Mara is both *instructional* and *facilitative* as she and John *collaborate* in finalizing the plan for algebra program improvement that will be taken to the Curriculum Council for approval.

7. Mara leads John through a *facilitative, transformational* coaching role play to prepare him for difficult conversations with the few parents and teachers who oppose the changes.

8. Back where they started in the blended coaching dance, Mara takes a *facilitative* approach in leading a conversation in which John reflects upon how those difficult conversations went, upon progress to date, and upon possible next steps.

In the chapters that follow, we explore Blended Coaching Strategies in more depth, and we examine the ways in which effective coaches and coachees dance their way around the Möbius strip.

7

Facilitative Coaching

Facilitative coaching builds upon a coachee's existing skills, knowledge, interpretations, and beliefs—and helps the coachee construct new skills, knowledge, interpretations, and beliefs that will form the basis for future actions. The coach does not focus on sharing professional expert knowledge. Rather, he or she uses facilitative methods to support the coachee in developing the capacity to build expertise through self-actualized reflective practice. In facilitative coaching the locus of control leans toward the coachee. A facilitative coach does not make his or her own assessments the center of the conversation but leads the coachee to form and examine his or her own assessments. The coach helps the coachee to gather and interpret data and feedback, develop his or her own interpretations, and analyze and select courses of action.

OUTCOMES OF FACILITATIVE COACHING

Facilitative coaching strategies can have a number of positive outcomes.

Creating New Possibilities by Taking a Fresh Look at Assertions and Assessments. Our assessments shape our future behaviors and define the possibilities we allow ourselves. Educators certainly know this; the impact of teacher expectations on student achievement, for example, is very well documented.

> I give up. It's no use even trying to get Mr. Jones to help his students be more successful. I've talked to him. I've sent him to workshops. I arranged for him to visit a model classroom. He says the kids are too lazy. The bottom line is, *he's* lazy. He's doesn't want any extra work. He wants to take the easy way out every time.

In this case, the principal is assessing Mr. Jones' resistance to change as a case of laziness. While there might be some truth in this, we could probably find plenty of evidence—stated in the form of assertions—that this teacher, who works without breaks with 33 fifth graders five days a week, is not lazy by most standards. Mr. Jones' behavior could be assessed and interpreted in a number of ways. By dismissing Mr. Jones as lazy, this principal is limiting her own ability to support Mr. Jones' professional development.

Her coach might ask how she has supported Mr. Jones, and how her assessment of Mr. Jones as lazy might have influenced his receptivity. Might she have inadvertently communicated her assessment to Mr. Jones? How might her assessment of him as a lazy man express low expectations and thus limit the likelihood that he will change his behaviors? What other assessments might be considered that could allow for a more productive future? For example, if it is insecurity rather than laziness that keeps Mr. Jones from holding high expectations for himself and for his students, what kind of support might help Mr. Jones to grow as a professional?

A facilitative coach intervenes by helping a coachee reexamine existing data, gather and evaluate new data, and explore unquestioned assessments. Through this process, which involves questioning, spotlighting data, and providing feedback, the coach challenges the coachee to refine her thinking and develop new interpretations and possibilities for action.

Developing Problem-Solving Skills. Through facilitative questions, the coach helps the coachee define and evaluate problems and solutions. The coaching conversation also models the problem-solving language and process that school administrators can use with groups they lead. Looking at a problem from various angles before reaching a conclusion or solution is a skill that will help the principal be a strong facilitator for problem solving and decision making. The coach can ask, "How might you get more information about this teacher's skills and knowledge? How could we help this teacher take the first steps toward improvement? How can we build on the teacher's strengths to help him move forward?" The coaching session can end with a plan of action that includes next steps and a plan for evaluating their impact. The coachee moves from being stuck with a no-win assessment to a renewed sense of empowerment and a clear action plan.

Building Self-Reflective Practice. A fundamental goal of facilitative coaching is to build the habits of mind that constitute reflective practice. A facilitative coach mediates the process of acquiring these habits. Conversations between coach and coachee serve as a model for the internal dialogues of a self-reflective practitioner. This makes it possible for the coachee to challenge her own assessments, perceptions, ideas, and actions. A self-reflective practitioner attempts to understand events and situations, including how she is perceived by others, from multiple perspectives. She has internalized the plan-act-reflect cycle at the micro and macro levels.

Shifting the Locus of Control From Coach to Coachee. Linked to the goal of building self-reflective practice in the coachee is the long-term goal of shifting the locus of control in the coaching relationship from the coach to the coachee. As novices, we don't know what we don't know, and we rely on our coaches to help us identify our needs and next steps. As we gain experience, we still benefit from the discipline and outside perspective that comes with coaching, while at the same time we have the internal resources to guide our own professional growth.

APPLYING FACILITATIVE STRATEGIES

Facilitative coaching can only occur if a trusting relationship has been built between coach and coachee. When the coachee is comfortable with the coach and is willing to be open about beliefs, assessments, and observations, facilitative coaching can produce powerful learning. However, before launching into a facilitative session, the coach must determine whether the issues at hand hold the promise of fruitful learning when balanced against constraints posed by time. Is it an urgent issue that must be taken care of immediately, or can it be addressed over time?

A leadership coach is not in a position to help a coachee work through every single problem as soon as it presents itself. Instead, there should be a triage process in place to determine which issues are to be acknowledged and set aside, which are to be tackled quickly and directly, and which are best addressed through facilitative processes over time. These include the deeper issues that promise big payoffs. This process can be informed by tools such as 360° survey instruments, self-assessments, and goals statements developed for internal or external evaluators.

A reflective conversation in which the coach maintains a facilitative stance may not be the most efficient way to share information, but it is a powerful means to support the development of leadership capacity. Successful facilitative coaching rests upon the assumption that the coachee possesses or can independently acquire the skills, knowledge, and dispositions required to resolve a question or need. A reflective conversation about rewriting the school plan will not go far if the novice has little knowledge or experience in relation to the mechanics and regulatory aspects of the school planning process.

On the other hand, let's suppose the coachee grasps the technical requirements she must meet in rewriting the plan. What she doesn't understand is that a school plan can be a tool for school improvement. She is looking at the plan revision simply as a project she will complete—without significant input—to bring her school into compliance. The coach, however, recognizes the plan as an opportunity to build internal resources in the coachee as a culture builder and instructional leader. The coach knows that the principal must understand on some level that successful implementation of school processes and programs depends on data analysis, vision building, and stakeholder engagement. The coach sees that using a facilitative approach will help the principal grasp the connection between revising the plan and improving the school, and emerge as an instructional leader.

PRINCIPAL: "Maybe you could help me get my plan revision done. You could read my draft."

COACH: "Sure. Tell me what you are trying to accomplish here."

PRINCIPAL: "Well, it's an update I have to turn in to the district and the State Department of Education. The teachers are busy with the new math adoption and report cards."

COACH: "Sounds like you want to rewrite the plan yourself and shelter your teachers from the work."

PRINCIPAL: "That's where I am headed, though maybe there will be less buy-in if I 'shelter' them."

COACH: "I am wondering what your priority is here—getting the plan done without creating stress for your staff, or using the plan as a tool for moving your school."

PRINCIPAL: "Maybe I do need to find a way to involve staff in the process. How could I use the plan revision to bring the faculty together in a powerful way, but without overwhelming them?"

COACH: "Great question! Let's think about what a more inclusive process would look like, one in which your vision was out in front."

BASIC MOVES OF FACILITATIVE COACHING

Facilitative coaching is a deceptively simple process that leads a coachee through a reflective conversation by questioning, paraphrasing, and summarizing. Table 7.1 outlines five basic moves in facilitative coaching and provides sample language stems for each.

Table 7.1   Five Moves in Facilitative Coaching

Paraphrasing	"So . . .?" "In other words . . ." "You're saying that . . ."
Clarifying questions	"To what extent . . .?" "It would help me if you would give me an example." "Let me see if I understand . . ." "Tell me what you mean when you . . ."
Paraphrasing with interpretation	"What you are describing could mean . . ." "Based on what you have described so far . . ." "Tell me if what you are saying means that . . ."
Mediational questions	"What's another way you might . . .?" "What would it look like if . . .?" "How might she react if . . .?" "What might be his rationale for . . .?"
Summarizing statements	"Let's review the key points of the discussion. "Can you describe your next steps?"

Adapted from Gilley & Broughton 1996, pp. 136–141.

Paraphrasing

In paraphrasing, the coach restates the speaker's message—"Let me see if I understand"—to test his own understanding and the speaker's clarity. When the speaker hears his own message restated by the listener, the speaker has the opportunity to evaluate it and become aware of how it is being heard.

PRINCIPAL: "So we had our first meeting to brainstorm strategies to improve our literacy program. Things went well. We got a lot done. The seventh-grade team was off task, but the rest of them were great."

COACH: "So, you were pleased with the outcomes of the meeting but have a concern about the participation of the seventh-grade team."

As simple as it may seem, paraphrasing is a powerful technique. It forces the speaker out of his own head. Most of us speak most of the time in generalities that reveal unrefined thinking. When we hear our language reflected back to us by a listener, we are stimulated to fine-tune our thinking as well as our speaking.

Clarifying Questions

Clarifying questions are essential to facilitative coaching for several reasons. First, they are key to the process of identifying the needs of the coachee and the nature of the issues at hand. The coach can use them to lead the coachee through a process of discovery as the coachee is asked to think more precisely and deeply about a given issue.

Clarifying questions also forestall the tendency to move directly and perhaps too hastily to a solution, as they offer the coachee the rare opportunity to think for more than a few seconds about any one topic. They also extend the coach's opportunity to listen to the coachee's language and uncover underlying issues, feelings, and attitudes. When the coach asks, "Can you explain what you mean by . . . ," the coachee will restate or revise his words and be more likely to reveal his attitudes and beliefs as a result.

Clarifying questions can also lead coachees to find connections between ideas as well as to develop and maintain focus. In response to "What is important about . . . ," it is not unusual for a coachee to answer with "Now that I've thought about . . . ," and shift his perspective on the issue.

PRINCIPAL: "The seventh-grade team is just always a step behind everyone else."

COACH: "Can you give me a few examples of this?"

Clarifying questions help coachees gather and interpret data and are powerful tools for pushing them to examine their assessments. Asking, "How do you know that?" or, "What evidence do you have to support that judgment?" moves the coachee away from unspoken assumptions and brings ideas to the surface so they can be examined more readily. Spending enough time paraphrasing and asking clarifying questions are essential steps to take before moving more deeply into facilitative coaching or deciding to shift to instructional coaching.

Paraphrasing With Interpretation

In paraphrasing with interpretation, a coach goes beyond restating his understanding of a coachee's utterance. He inserts his own perspective and tests ideas or interpretations with the coachee. By bringing a different lens, background knowledge, and experiences to the conversation, the coach can assist the coachee by offering new ways to represent herself and her concerns.

PRINCIPAL: "Let's see. There's the body language. They give each other looks and do some eye rolling when certain suggestions are made. Then they have inside jokes and laugh about things that the rest of us don't know about. Then they usually bring paperwork to complete during the meetings so they aren't really attentive to what's going on."

COACH: "Sounds like there are patterns of behavior that have been established within their small group that sidetrack your process and that they feel free to exhibit in the larger group."

Mediational Questions

Mediational questions are crafted in order to produce a shift in thinking. Costa and Garmston (2002) describe a "mediator" as one who comes between another person and a *task* or between another person and *meaning*. The mediator—for our purposes, the coach—influences the direction and flow of another person's thinking through conversation. The coach listens for what the coachee understands and articulates—but with an ear tuned for what the coachee *isn't* saying. Sometimes coachees aren't forthright because they are unwilling to expose vulnerabilities. At other times coachees tell it as they see it but are limited by their own experiences and perspective.

By exploring past actions using a question such as "What would it have looked like if . . . ?," the coach can help the coachee analyze what worked or didn't work and compare and contrast what was planned with what ensued. By posing future-oriented questions—"What would it look like if . . . ?" or "What's another way you might . . . ?"—the coach can guide the thinking of the coachee in new directions into unexplored territory, and the coachee can generate or imagine new possibilities. By asking, "How would . . . be different from . . . ?," the coach pushes the coachee to compare and contrast ideas, which helps the coachee understand a situation from various points of view. Through mediational questioning, the coach encourages the development of the coachee's problem analysis skills. Being able and willing to analyze a situation thoroughly before moving into action is an essential skill for school leaders and one of the central skills developed through the coaching process.

PRINCIPAL: "Yes. This goes on at every meeting. We wrote out meeting norms at the beginning of the year—but that didn't help much."

COACH: "What would it look like if you were to build those norms into your culture?"

PRINCIPAL: "Well, as I said, they're posted—but we haven't really discussed them since we posted them. I think I need to bring them up at the beginning of each meeting. Or maybe what we need to do is reexamine them and decide how well they're working. This would get the teachers to point out how we could do better, and that would help everyone recommit to the norms."

Summarizing Statements

Coaching conversations can include many digressions, but they should be focused and goal oriented and progress smoothly from exploration to interpretation to commitment to action. Summarizing statements sustain this trajectory. Noting the key points, insights, or possible next steps, the coach can periodically bring these forward with summarizing statements such as "It sounds like you now think that . . ." or "Here's what we've covered so far. . . ." These statements allow the coachee to consider, revise, and refine what's been said. By sorting the key ideas from a lengthy conversation, the coach helps the coachee organize thoughts so they can more easily be analyzed and evaluated. Summarizing questions—"Can you describe your next steps?"—encourage the coachee to master this mental process of sorting and prioritizing. Thus, summarizing helps the coachee maintain focus and clarity, pinpoint next steps, and review commitments.

COACH: "Well, in the past several minutes you've mentioned a few things. Let's write down those you can commit to as action steps."

PRINCIPAL: "OK. I'm going to put a discussion of the norms on the next meeting agenda with the goal of recommitting or modifying them if necessary. Then for the rest of the year, I'll start each meeting by reviewing them. I wonder what else we could do to make it work."

You can see how the facilitative conversation shifts as the coach and the coachee identify areas that need clarification or exploration. Once a few action steps are determined, it can still be useful to refine them by posing additional clarifying and mediation questions. This may create even more possibilities for action. The coach might ask, "How do you think the faculty will respond to revisiting the norms? What indications do you have that the group would support active implementation of positive meeting norms? How do you think you could involve some teacher leaders in this process?" The coach supports the principal's success by listening carefully, asking probing questions, and encouraging the coachee to reflect, ground assessments, explore new possibilities, and commit to productive next steps.

What might have happened in our vignette if this principal had been unfamiliar with processes for using meeting norms? What if our principal were unfamiliar with processes for coming to consensus? What does a coach do when the conversation stops because the principal lacks the necessary knowledge or skills to move forward? To support principals in building their knowledge and skills, coaches must be prepared to use instructional strategies.

8

Instructional Coaching

From studies of learning in and out of school, it appears that people build up knowledge by solving real problems using available clues, tools and social supports. Traditional apprenticeships provide one model of this kind of learning. In an apprenticeship, a beginner develops flexible skills and conditional knowledge by working on genuine tasks in the company of a master. Take, for example, the situated and sequenced process by which apprentice tailors learn to produce garments. From observing masters, apprentices develop an image of how an entire garment is produced while they work on specific components (e.g., a sleeve) and practice specific skills (e.g., cutting, pressing, using the sewing machine). In such an apprenticeship, knowing cannot be separated from doing.

Sharon Feiman-Nemser and Janine Remillard,
authors of *Perspectives on Learning to Teach*

School leadership coaches have to be prepared to teach, to share their expertise and professional resources with their coachees. When a school leader has the requisite knowledge and skills, we often use facilitative strategies to help the coachee deepen understandings and think through options for action. However, there are times when a more direct approach is appropriate. In these cases the coach must take on an instructional role.

Instructional coaching is an approach in which the coach shares his or her own experience, expertise, and craft wisdom with the coachee by using traditional teaching strategies. These may include modeling, providing resources, and direct instruction. The intended outcomes remain the same: to support the coachee in clarifying and committing to appropriate goals and in taking effective action. In instructional coaching, the coach provides what the coachee may lack. In Blended Coaching, instructional coaching is usually nested in facilitative coaching as coaches work with coachees to assess needs and as coachees develop understandings and start to apply what they know.

As we have noted, the principalship is a highly complex job that demands the mastery of a multitude of skills and areas of knowledge. Principals are expected to know it all and to know it now. An effective coach can make a significant difference in the success of principals and other school leaders, particularly novices, by providing them with "just in time" instructional coaching.

APPLICATIONS OF INSTRUCTIONAL COACHING

Time is almost always of the essence in the principalship. When it is clear that the coachee does not possess the knowledge or internal resources required for action, and when that action must be taken quickly, instructional coaching is often the most effective strategy. Sometimes a coachee's needs are simple and operational. For example, a principal may need to know state guidelines for counting instructional minutes and how to use a template to keep track of them. At other times the needs might be more complex. A principal with no background in bilingual education may need to evaluate several bilingual teachers. In both cases, the principal can immediately benefit from professional knowledge, resources, or direction provided by the coach.

Reflection: Why would instructional coaching be the right move in the following situation?

COACH: "How is your planning coming for your opening staff meeting?"

COACHEE: "Pretty well. One thing I want to do is review our spring test data."

COACH: "How will you go about this? What do you want to accomplish?"

COACHEE: "I'm not sure. First off, I've got binders full of printouts, but I am not sure how to interpret or present the results. Also, I want to do more than just pass out numbers, but I am not sure just how to proceed."

BACKGROUND KNOWLEDGE AND PROCESS SKILLS

Principals must be able to perform fairly simple and clear-cut tasks such as filling out forms and following timelines. They are also responsible for highly sophisticated tasks such as meeting facilitation and problem solving. Each type of task is challenging in its own way; taken together, they can be overwhelming. Completing them requires both background knowledge and process skills.

Background knowledge is what one must know, and process skills are what one must be able to do. Knowledge and skills are fairly distinct, and both are critical to effectiveness. In order to provide leadership in implementing the IEP process at her site, for example, a principal should possess knowledge about special education law and programs, and process skills for facilitating meetings, problem solving, and conflict resolution. Unpacking the knowledge and skills required to accomplish a task or goal is a way of focusing the coaching process.

Background and technical knowledge are usually specific and may be efficiently developed through instructional coaching. The coach can hand the coachee sample surveys, copies of meeting norms, information about group processes, and even articles describing tools and processes for collecting and analyzing survey data. However, we cannot assume the principal has the process skills required for effective implementation. Through facilitative coaching, the coach must probe to find out what process skills the principal has and then move again into instructional coaching to provide the principal with the skills required to achieve success.

Table 8.1   Completed Analysis of Knowledge and Skills Template

In order to DESIGN A MEETING in which the faculty analyzes survey data

- A principal must know (background knowledge)
  - ✓ Elements of effective meetings
  - ✓ Small and large group discussion processes
  - ✓ Meeting norms
  - ✓ Elements of effective surveys
  - ✓ Background about the school/community relationships
  - ✓ Background about previous use of surveys at this school

- A principal must know how to (process skills)
  - ✓ Design and communicate the agenda
  - ✓ Share leadership
  - ✓ Encourage positive norms
  - ✓ Facilitate meetings
  - ✓ Facilitate interpretation of data
  - ✓ Facilitate discussion and decision making

Table 8.2   Sample Analysis of Knowledge and Skills Template

*In order to*_____

- A principal must know (Background knowledge)
  - ✓ _____
  - ✓ _____
  - ✓ _____
  - ✓ _____
  - ✓ _____
  - ✓ _____

- A principal must know how to (Process skills)
  - ✓ _____
  - ✓ _____
  - ✓ _____
  - ✓ _____
  - ✓ _____
  - ✓ _____

Exercise: Use the template in Table 8.2 to practice analyzing the background knowledge and the process skills needed to complete the following tasks:

- Lead the revision of the school plan
- Hire a new language arts teacher
- Set up the master schedule (secondary) or class configurations (elementary)
- Supervise and evaluate a teacher
- Analyze assessment data

AVOIDING "WAR STORIES"

A coach can offer personal thoughts and experiences that support, reassure, and motivate the coachee. However, coaches must resist the temptation to turn coaching into the sharing of "war stories." There is no evidence to suggest that hearing the travails of a veteran will help another administrator move forward with his own situation. Coaches should remember that adults will resist anything they see as an attack on their competence. Storytelling and advice giving can put coachees on the defensive if they come to the conclusion that the coach's situation is different from their own; if they believe the coach does not understand their unique situation; or if they interpret the coach's success story as conveying superiority.

GETTING PERMISSION TO INSTRUCT

Even novice principals are seen as experts by their stakeholders. Principals are very aware that they must appear both knowledgeable and competent. Though a highly trained, responsible educator, the principal may feel insecure about new challenges and may be reluctant to admit any lack of knowledge or skills: "I was an English teacher and program coordinator. If I admit I really don't know much about mathematics programs, what will the folks in the math department think?" To ensure that the coachee is comfortable with the role of "learner," the coach asks for consent before moving into in-depth instructional coaching. This can be done simply by asking questions such as:

Would you like more information about . . .?

Would you like to spend some time looking at . . .?

Would you like me to describe some options for you?

Here is an example of how the process of asking for permission might take place, with a useful phrase highlighted.

PRINCIPAL: "So I'm doing my formal observation of my English as a Second Language teacher and when I went in to observe a lesson, she was speaking almost entirely in Spanish. They were talking about the seasons, and she had picture cards and words in English—but they were talking about their experiences in Spanish—so almost the entire lesson was taking place in Spanish."

COACH: "Can you describe what you expected to see?"

PRINCIPAL: "Well, that's where I'm just not sure. I'm not really sure exactly what portion of the lesson should be in Spanish. But it seems like if she is going to teach English, she should be speaking more English."

COACH: *"Would it be helpful to review the research* on language acquisition and to look at some model ESL lessons?"

PRINCIPAL: "Yes! And do you have those in writing so that I could share them with my teachers?"

Once the coachee accepts an invitation to learn new information, skills, or tools, the coach can proceed—ever mindful of the need to monitor and adjust based on the coachee's needs and responses.

As an experienced administrator, the coach may know "just what to do" in a particular situation. But he must proceed carefully, using language that keeps the new information, skills, or tools away from his personal experience base and his own ego. Avoid the sentence stems such as "I used to . . ." or "Once, I . . ." so the coachee is able to reject a suggestion without putting herself in the position of embarrassing or disagreeing with her coach. Notice how the following sentence stems keep the coach's identity and ego out of the conversation:

> There are a number of approaches that might work.
>
> There are a number of appropriate strategies.
>
> Should we investigate how Marge has approached this?
>
> Most practitioners believe that . . .
>
> Some principals have tried . . . and it might work for you.
>
> It might be helpful to . . .
>
> A couple of things to keep in mind are . . .
>
> The research on this suggests that . . .

Again, useful phrases are highlighted below:

PRINCIPAL: "You know there have been a lot of comments about our faculty meetings taking too long, so at my faculty meeting for this Thursday, I'm trying out my new style of agenda. We're designating who will lead each item, and we're stating the number of minutes that item can take. I ran it by my leadership team and they think it's a great idea. I'm hoping this new structure can keep the meeting under control."

COACH: "Having the number of minutes each item can take is really helpful. *Some principals* also have a timekeeper who gives a one- or two-minute warning when time is almost up."

PRINCIPAL: "That's a good idea . . . I think that would really work here."

COACH: "*Sometimes* that role is shared or *sometimes* there's one person who is particularly good at it and who wants to do it all the time."

PRINCIPAL: "Oh, I have someone who would be great at that and I know she'd really like that job. She was one of the most concerned about the meetings lasting too long."

COACH: "Have you thought about how you might evaluate the success of this new process?"

MOVING BETWEEN INSTRUCTIONAL AND FACILITATIVE COACHING

A typical coaching session shifts fluidly between facilitative and instructional approaches. The coach may move briefly into instructional coaching—to offer new information or point out something the coachee has missed—and then return to facilitative coaching once the coachee has the knowledge that is needed to proceed.

COACH: "What's been working well for you?"

PRINCIPAL: "I got to attend the Every Child Succeeds Conference—and got lots of ideas."

COACH: "What ideas are foremost in your thinking right now?"

PRINCIPAL: "Well, they talked about how important it is to have a two-hour literacy block. So I looked at our bell schedule, and if I move recess by ten minutes, we can do it. Since we don't have a faculty meeting for another two weeks, I thought I'd just go ahead and put it in our Monday bulletin so that we can get started right away—so that's pretty much worked out. I'm excited about having a stronger focus on literacy."

COACH: "Can we spend a few minutes thinking about that change in bell schedule and what some of the initial reactions and responses might be when teachers find out about it via a memo?"

PRINCIPAL: "Uh-oh. Is this one of those land mines?"

COACH: "It could be! There are a few things to keep in mind as you decide which decisions you'll make by yourself, and which you'll take to the faculty. In general, the more directly a change affects the classroom, the more teachers will want to be part of the discussion and decision."

PRINCIPAL: "I suppose I could ruffle some feathers here."

COACH: "So let's think about teachers who have been accustomed to planning instruction in certain time blocks for several years. How might they respond if you issue a change in schedule through a memo . . . with no discussion?"

PRINCIPAL: "OK. I get it. I can think of a few teachers already who might get really upset . . . let me go get those memos before the teachers see them. Then I'd like to plan out how to approach this change."

COACH: "And let's start with your vision for a literacy block. How would you like to see that time used? What would it take to ensure that quality instruction was taking place in every classroom during this chunk of time?"

9

Collaborative Coaching

> Janet is a principal who has just returned from a district meeting. She received a packet of information about conducting a self-study for a Coordinated Compliance Review (CCR) of state and federal categorical programs. She has the timeline and list of tasks—but is overwhelmed and has no idea how to start, what the process should look like, how she should or shouldn't involve staff, and what the outcome of the self-study should be. She's in the middle of rewriting her school improvement plan and isn't sure how or whether to integrate these processes.

In this typical scenario, the principal possesses a significant amount of knowledge about the school's categorical programs, and she understands the practical aspects of completing a self-study that meets program requirements. What is difficult for her to sort out is the role that the self-study could play in the larger scheme of her school improvement processes. She would benefit from facilitative coaching as she prioritizes tasks and makes a plan to take advantage of the CCR process to support moving her school toward the realization of its vision. She will also benefit from her coach's experience in managing large and complex projects that span several months, are data driven, and require the participation of stakeholders.

This scenario presents an opportunity for what we call *collaborative coaching.* This strategy falls between the core strategies of instruction and facilitation because the coach is constantly in both modes throughout a project that is collaborative in nature. The coach gets his hands dirty and does at least some portion of the work alongside the coachee. The focus is on concrete action with a larger goal to develop knowledge, skills, and internal capacity that can be generalized to other situations. In the case we have outlined above, Janet and her coach might sit down and jointly develop a plan for conducting the self-study and completing the school plan. The coach might help Janet develop a presentation outlining the school's progress in increasing student achievement. He might also review Janet's self-study and plan documents.

USES OF COLLABORATIVE COACHING

Collaborative coaching is appropriate when the coach and coachee have identified a need or problem conducive to shared work that promises to generate powerful learning for the coachee. This strategy is not about a coach rescuing an overwhelmed coachee by doing the coachee's job. It is applicable when a clear project or task is identified—such as evaluating the effectiveness of a literacy program, planning a specific meeting agenda, writing a difficult letter or evaluation, or setting up budget processes. In these examples, the coach and coachee each possess pieces of what is required to complete the project. One without the other couldn't meet the need—but via collaborative coaching, the plan or product developed by the principal will be better than what would have been achieved working in isolation. In an effective collaborative project, the coach brings expertise, resources, and perspective, while the coachee brings intimate knowledge of the situation and the positional authority to implement actions.

Collaborative coaching is not appropriate if the process would undermine the authority and image of the coachee. The coach must be sensitive to the way the coachee perceives their relationship and responds to coaching. Does the principal tend to give up power when the coach "takes over"? If this is the case, then it is best to stick to facilitative coaching strategies. But when the coachee feels confident about what she brings to the table and seeks to use the expertise and assistance of the coach to help accomplish clear goals, the collaboration can move forward productively.

AN EXAMPLE OF COLLABORATIVE COACHING

In the following example, the principal and coach recognize the need to revitalize the governance structure at Wisconsin High.

PRINCIPAL: "The school board has asked us to review the core reading lists for our English classes and submit a new set of recommendations."

COACH: "Can you give me some background on this issue?"

PRINCIPAL: "We've been getting a lot of challenges lately, parents complaining about books like *Catcher in the Rye*, and some undercurrents against some of the modern selections on our lists like *House on Mango Street* and *Beloved*."

COACH: "Tell me how you would like this review process to play out."

PRINCIPAL: "Well, I'd like to be inclusive, but I don't want to open Pandora's box. And I want the professionals to have the final say."

COACH: "What kind of structures does the school have in place for this sort of decision making?"

PRINCIPAL: "Not much. There are the department chairs and department meetings, and on the parent side there are some booster clubs. The previous principal let the parent council die a quiet death, and I don't think that students have ever had a voice in curriculum issues. And I haven't got a clue how to juggle all of these groups."

COACH: "Sounds like you would like to develop a clearer, more inclusive governance structure here, and this reading list issue provides the rationale for you to take this on.

COACHEE: "Absolutely."

COACH: "It might be a good use of our time to put our heads together on this issue. Would you be interested in my help designing a governance model for Wisconsin?"

In collaborative coaching the coach may offer an array of approaches or solutions to the issue being addressed. But the coachee determines the processes and tools that will best match her school. It is critical that the coach not push a particular remedy onto the coachee, but let her articulate the unique needs and select the best solution. It is the principal who will step out alone in front of the stakeholders with the plan or product of collaboration—and the principal must fully own it. In the beginning, the coach might be in the lead, but by the end of the collaboration, the coachee should be firmly holding the reins.

Table 9.1   Collaborative Coaching Scenario: Governance

Wisconsin High		
Step 1	The need is identified by the coachee and clarified through the coaching process.	*The principal wants to bring an inclusive process to an instructional issue, but there is no structure in place. She lacks experience in this area and requests the coach's support.*
Step 2	The coachee sets the outcome and agrees to collaborate.	*The principal articulates her goal and vision with the support of the coach. The coach agrees to work with the principal to develop a governance structure model and to assist the principal in shepherding its implementation.*
Step 3	The coach shares available resources and ideas and poses questions and suggestions.	*The coach shares research and articles on high school governance. He identifies high schools in the region with successful governance models and puts the coachee in touch with the principals of those schools. He arranges a meeting between himself, the principal, and the superintendent to clarify understanding of the district's expectations.*
Step 4	The coachee selects resources, clarifies needs, and accepts/rejects/modifies the options generated in conversation between coach and coachee.	*Together, the principal and coach identify the characteristics of a model that would work best for the school. Together they generate options for a structure that includes parent, staff, and student advisory bodies and outlines suggestions for their respective roles. The coach drafts several organizational charts for the principal to review and to share with others.*
Step 5	The coach and coachee work together to support the implementation of the project.	*The principal agrees to the formation of several advisory groups. The coach and principal draft a task-analysis and timeline for the creation of the structure and for the implementation of the core reading review process.*

Table 9.1 (Continued)

Step 6	The coach continues to draw attention to gaps, offer resources, and refine the thinking and decisions of the coachee through listening, observing, questioning, and providing feedback.	*The implementation of the governance structure is the subject of ongoing review over the course of the year. The coach attends several parent advisory meetings for the purpose of providing feedback to the principal.*
Step 7	The coachee makes the final decisions about the product and the process.	*The buck always stops at the principal's desk. The coach leads the principal through a "cycle of inquiry" process around the implementation of the governance model, guiding the principal as she selects next steps.*

10

Consultative Coaching

Consultative coaching is a particular form of instructional coaching that relies upon specific expertise a coach can bring to a coaching relationship. Peter Block defines a consultant as "a person in a position to have some influence over an individual, a group, or an organization, but who has no direct power to make changes or implement programs" (2000, p. 2). In contrast to collaborative coaching, in the consultative mode a coach shares perspective, knowledge, and advice, but does not own or participate in any action that results from the coaching process.

Consultative coaching focuses on specific areas relating to school programs or processes, usually of a technical nature. The coach-as-consultant possesses resources or expertise that will benefit the coachee and her school. In addition to sharing knowledge and resources, the consultative coach might carry out data gathering on behalf of the coachee and may provide specific recommendations in particular situations.

John is concerned because achievement data for his eighth-grade students indicate a discrepancy between their language and math scores. The data show that aggregate scores in language consistently drop during the three years that students spend in John's school. In his efforts to figure out what is going on, he has visited the school's English and social studies classrooms many times. He sees well-managed classrooms taught by experienced teachers. He has a few ideas as to what might be going on; he suspects that there is a need for more differentiated instruction, but by and large, he is stumped by the unsatisfactory scores. He asks his coach, a highly successful middle school principal in a former life, for assistance.

BASIC STEPS IN CONSULTATIVE COACHING

Determine the need and agree upon a consultative approach. In this example, the principal—John—shares his data with the coach and expresses his concerns. Using a facilitative approach, the coach helps John clarify the need. She then tells John that the area of need is one in which she has expertise and offers to provide consultative support. Once the two agree that she will serve in a consultant role on this problem, the coach works with John to gather additional data and to deepen her understanding of the situation. In this case, she will conduct classroom observations with John, examine test data, and review performance by teacher, year, and subgroup. Once she has a handle on what's happening in the classroom, she and John can discuss the school's dynamics, the history of instructional programs, and professional development prior to reviewing potential courses of action.

Provide advice, examples, and resources. Once they agree on the need, the coach, as expert, can provide resources and advice. It is helpful to set aside a specific time for this purpose during which it is made clear that the coach is playing a consultative role. In our example, the coach shares a data analysis showing that scores are being pulled down by declining achievement among students in the top and bottom quartiles. She shares several articles on differentiated instruction in literacy at the secondary level. They discuss options for approaching these issues in light of the school's particular needs. The coach recommends potential action steps to the principal, including conducting an analysis of achievement data with the staff, creating a professional development plan, and establishing accelerated and intervention curricula in newly created student groupings.

Extend support beyond the one-to-one coaching relationship. The consultative coach can support the implementation and evaluation of program improvements in a variety of ways. As long as the role is explicit, short term, and based in the area of the coach's expertise, the consultative coach can engage with staff and others in the consultant role. In this example, the coach agrees to conduct a mini-workshop for John and his leadership team in which they will analyze the assessment data. She also suggests that the leadership team visit several other schools in the region and arranges for those visitations.

THE RISKS OF CONSULTATIVE COACHING

Consultative coaching is an approach to be applied with restraint. Its overuse can build dependency—and *independence* is what coaching is intended to foster. A coach in the consultative role can easily undermine a coachee's confidence and professional growth by being patronizing or prescriptive. Imposing a particular style of leadership or specific practices that aren't chosen by the principal can be disempowering and unproductive. Furthermore, coaches can be wrong in their analysis and recommendations. Coachees may hesitate to challenge the advice because they look up to, and respect, their coaches.

Coaches must also be knowledgeable about and careful to respect established practices and district philosophy. When projects are visible to the school community and the principal doesn't really own them but attributes them instead to the coach, the authority of the principal can be undermined in the eyes of stakeholders. In addition, when problems or conflicts come up, the coach may be targeted for blame by stakeholders and by the principal. Of course, the coach may receive all the credit if things go well. Either way, the coaching relationship as well as the credibility of the principal can be damaged in a way that runs counter to the goals of coaching.

Reflection: What are areas in which you possess the expertise to provide consultative coaching? What are some areas in which you should resist any temptation to provide consultative support?

11

Transformational Coaching

Succeeding as a school leader is not just about what you know. It is also about who you are. Leadership coaches must be prepared to support their coachees in their struggles with difficult personal issues as well as their acquisition of new knowledge and skills. This is why the right side of our Möbius strip includes an approach to facilitative coaching that we refer to as *transformational coaching.*

We have discussed the critical importance of interpersonal and communication skills, cultural proficiency, and emotional intelligence in effective school leadership. While there are cognitive dimensions to each of these performance areas, they must also be addressed in terms of the deeper, less malleable, and more change-resistant domains of disposition and personality, the internal inclinations that constitute our ways of being.

In *The Leadership Challenge,* James Kouzes and Barry Posner outline five practices common to successful leaders, maintaining that they "challenge the process, inspire a shared vision, enable others to act, model the way, and encourage the heart" (1987, p. 8). Influencing school leaders to increase their effectiveness in these domains is the most difficult form of coaching, as we are helping our coachees change *who they are.* This poses different challenges from simply teaching someone new knowledge and skills.

Can people learn new ways of being, or are our personalities, dispositions, and interpersonal skills fixed? If you are going to serve as a coach, you need to be very clear in your response to this question. Effective coaches believe firmly that people are capable of making fundamental internal changes. Research on these questions is consistent with common sense. Recent studies, particularly studies of identical twins raised separately, indicate that a big part of who we are is genetically determined. In fact, it is estimated that about 50 percent of what is commonly called personality is fixed in our genes. It is not unusual for twins raised in different environments to end up in similar professions and to have similar tastes and identical gestures and idiosyncrasies.

Dispositions, personality, and interpersonal skills are not fixed, however. Environment and experience play major roles in determining these in each of us. While we may not be able to alter the half of who we are that is determined by nature, there is plenty of room to maneuver on the side that is influenced by nurture. And the principalship provides tremendous opportunities for learning new ways of being, for expanding one's repertoire of possibilities.

Here are a few examples of ways in which experienced principals report they have been personally transformed through their work:

"When I first entered administration, I had little confidence in myself, and I rarely spoke up at management meetings. When I did speak up, it was only after mentally rehearsing every word I was going to say. Now I am recognized as a leader among my peers and they can't shut me up!"

"I am an introvert. I dread schmoozing at school parties or the Rotary luncheon. But I had to learn to do it to succeed in the job, and now I sometimes find myself really enjoying it."

"For years I avoided raising concerns I had with some of my teachers. I was afraid of conflict, afraid of damaging my relationship with these teachers and my reputation for being a nice guy. I have finally learned how to lay out my expectations and raise concerns comfortably."

"Every time the superintendent called with a parent complaint, I was a basket case. I was sure my job was on the line and that I had done something wrong. Now I understand that this comes with the territory and that every one of these interactions is a potential learning experience."

"I grew up in a white, middle-class home and went through schools that were less than diverse. But I studied Spanish in high school, and served in Guatemala in the Peace Corps. I'm principal of a school that serves mostly Mexican immigrants. I'm not Latino by birth or upbringing, but I believe that I am a genuinely bicultural person."

THE POWER OF TRANSFORMATION: TRIPLE-LOOP LEARNING

We have a colleague who rode her first "century," a one-hundred-miles-in one-day bike journey, at age 55. At this point in her life, she is not a 56-year-old woman who rides a bike; she is a 56-year-old *bicyclist*. Bicycling has become a part of her way of being.

Becoming a bicyclist did not happen overnight. It occurred through incremental steps over time, starting with short rides, encouragement from friends, increasing distances, and most important, the declaration, "I can and I will do this." Through this transformational process, our friend has not only become very fit; she is now a person who has a hard time imagining a life without bicycling.

The process of transformation typically progresses through three stages:

- We gain new knowledge, skills, or ways of acting, in incremental steps.
- As we experience success with these new ways of doing things, we begin to change our way of thinking; we imagine a new context for these incremental changes; and we begin to reframe our sense of possibilities.
- As our new knowledge, skills, and ways of acting become transparent to us—integral to who we are—and as we see the world differently, our learning is fully integrated. We are transformed.

In *Masterful Coaching,* Robert Hargrove (1995) describes this process as *triple-loop learning.* He defines transformational coaching as a process that moves people beyond improved performance (single-loop learning), to developing new ways of thinking (double-loop learning), and ultimately to changing their ways of being (triple-loop learning). This framework has also been used by Peter Senge (1990) and others to describe levels of organizational learning.

Single-loop learning occurs on the instructional side of the Möbius strip of Blended Coaching Strategies. It is the place where incremental improvement occurs, where learners try out new knowledge, skills, and strategies. Facilitative coaching strategies, on the other hand, are directed at producing double- and triple-loop learning. At the double-loop level, learners begin to reshape their patterns of thinking, internalize new possibilities, and practice taking on new challenges independently. At the triple-loop level, the learner has integrated the new learning and embraces a new identity in relation to the challenge at hand. When this analysis is taken from the individual to the institutional level, we talk about moving an organization from adopting new rules or procedures to developing new systems and—ultimately—building new cultures.

Figure 11.1   The Triple-Loop Learning Process

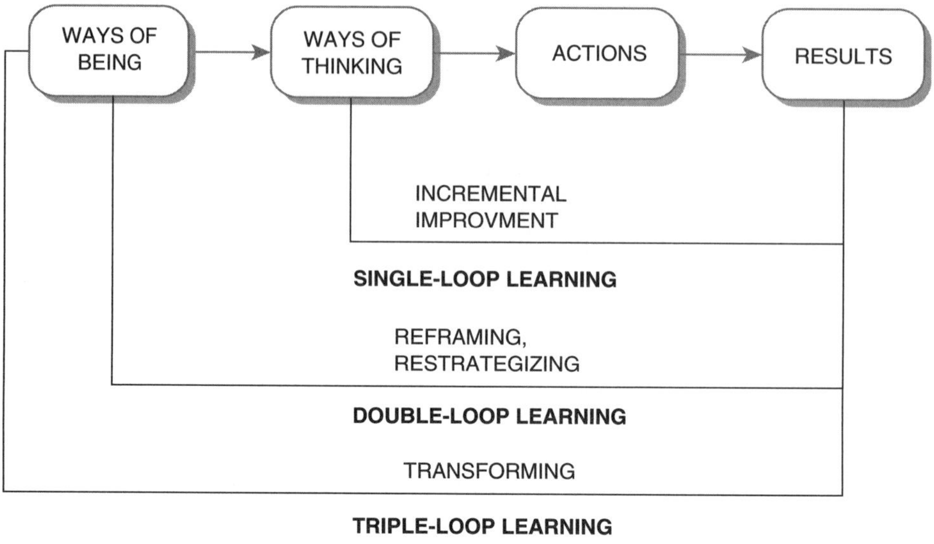

Triple Loop Learning Process, adapted from Hargrove, *Masterful Coaching*, p. 28.

Let's explore these concepts in relation to learning to play the piano. At the single-loop level, a learner might learn to tap out a few simple tunes from memory. At the double-loop level, a learner can read music with some fluency and is able to pick up new tunes, perhaps with some struggle, by reading music and practicing independently. At the triple-loop level, the learner is a musician—able to read, play, and compose with fluency and confidence. Figure 11.1 provides a schematic of the triple-loop learning process.

It is a dynamic one, and assumes that personal transformation is linked to and dependent on changes in how we act and what we think.

Table 11.1 provides several examples of triple-loop learning as it might apply to school principals.

ONTOLOGICAL COACHING AND COGNITIVE-BEHAVIORAL THERAPY: FOUNDATIONS FOR TRANSFORMATIONAL COACHING

Transformational coaching is informed by two closely related disciplines, *ontological coaching* and *cognitive-behavioral therapy*. Ontology is the study of being, and, in particular, the investigation of the nature of being human. In developing ontological coaching, Rafael Echeverría and Julio Olalla (1992) have examined the role of language in shaping human experience and

Table 11.1   Triple-Loop Learning Examples

SCENARIO 1: Latino parents are not involved in decision making at Suburban School. Kim has no experience with Latino students or communities.		
SINGLE-LOOP	*DOUBLE-LOOP*	*TRIPLE-LOOP*
Kim schedules site council meetings in the evening and provides child care in an effort to increase attendance.	Kim creates a Latino parent steering committee in order to develop meeting agendas and strategies for engaging parents.	Kim is relaxed when immersed in the Latino community. She seeks out opportunities to engage outside of the school setting. She is empathetic with recent immigrants and passionate in advocating for their interests.

SCENARIO 2: Jack avoids dealing with the school budget. He believes that he is "bad at math" and that the budget is "not about instruction."		
SINGLE-LOOP	*DOUBLE-LOOP*	*TRIPLE-LOOP*
Jack sits down with his secretary and reviews the budget.	Jack develops a monthly budget review and an annual budget planning process. He takes the school budget to the site council and staff for input.	Jack develops a deep understanding of the importance of aligning resources with his school vision. He asks difficult questions about how dollars are spent and develops systems for planning, evaluation, and allocation of funds. He is not intimidated by his multimillion-dollar budget.

SCENARIO 3: Formerly a teacher at Isla Negra School, Rick has recently been appointed to the principalship. Several teachers are not teaching the adopted curriculum. Rick is struggling with making the transition from colleague to leader.		
SINGLE-LOOP	*DOUBLE-LOOP*	*TRIPLE-LOOP*
Rick begins doing "quick visit" observations and asks teachers why they are not using the adopted materials.	Rick helps to create and facilitate grade-level planning groups that will support the implementation of the adopted curriculum.	Rick has a clear vision and expectations, and he communicates them consistently through processes such as professional development, school planning, and supervision. His personal identity has shifted to one of instructional leader among his former peers.

behavior. Building on the work of Humberto Maturana in the field of perception (Efran & Lukens, 1985) and the work of John Searle in linguistics (1969), Echeverría and Olalla illuminate the ways in which our interpretations of reality, embodied through language, shape our ways of being. A coach observes how individuals construct interpretations about their existence. An ontological coach helps individuals build new interpretations that open up new possibilities. In attending to our coachees' use of language and their interpretations of reality, we are able to provide a different perspective that may create opportunities for personal transformation.

Coaching is not therapy, as we have noted. However, as leadership coaches we have much to learn from professional therapists. The overall track record of talk therapy is questionable; some researchers maintain that talk therapy is no more effective over time than placebos or no treatment at all. The one form of talk therapy that produces fairly consistent positive outcomes, however, is cognitive-behavioral therapy. This is an approach that has much in common with ontological coaching and with what we call transformational coaching.

Cognitive-behavioral therapy assumes that maladaptive behaviors, moods, and emotions can result from ways of thinking and perceiving. This approach is based on the notion that the way in which an individual responds to a situation is shaped by "automatic thoughts," or learned responses, and personal interpretations. Cognitive therapists attempt to help patients recognize and change dysfunctional thinking patterns and replace undesirable behavior patterns with positive ones. This approach to therapy is congruent with the triple-loop learning model.

Ontological coaching and cognitive-behavioral therapy rely on conversations between the coach or therapist and the coachee or patient in order to disclose interpretations or thought patterns that are dysfunctional. Both disciplines also ask clients to try out new ways of being through exercises such as

- *Cognitive rehearsal.* The client imagines a problem situation and the coach or therapist guides him through a problem-solving process that leads to resolution.
- *Role-playing.* The therapist or coach constructs role plays that allow the client to experiment with new ways of being.
- *Validity testing.* Clients are asked to test the validity of their interpretations, providing evidence that they are true or false, functional or dysfunctional. Journals may be used in this process.
- *Homework assignments.* Clients are asked to try out ways of acting and being in the "real world."

How do these approaches link to Blended Coaching Strategies and to transformational coaching? As we work with our coachees to develop their capacity as school leaders, we often start in the instructional mode, at the level of single- and double-loop learning. But our goal has to be to move toward the deeper growth that is represented as triple-loop learning. Triple-loop learning requires the development of new ways of seeing and interpreting things and demands that we practice new ways of being. Developing new ways of seeing, interpreting, and being is at the heart of both ontological coaching and cognitive-behavioral therapy and forms the essence of transformational coaching.

Reflection: What might cognitive rehearsal, role-playing, validity testing, and homework look like in the context of leadership coaching?

THE BASIC MOVES OF TRANSFORMATIONAL COACHING

The ultimate goal of the coaching process is triple-loop learning and personal transformation. We hope to support the emergence of self-actualized leaders who have built internal capacity—self-reflective practitioners who take responsibility for their own professional growth. There are many models of what might be called transformational coaching in the literature. These frames may use different language, but generally they share the following common elements.

Start from breakdowns. Here we remind you once more of Michael Fullan's adage: "Problems are our friends" (1993, p. 21). Every conflict, failure to achieve a goal, or crisis of competence is a learning opportunity. When a coachee acknowledges a problem, that coachee creates an opening for the power of coaching.

Of course a coach must be selective, with input from the coachee, when determining which problems should be the focus of any coaching conversation. And it is critically important—as we point out in Chapter 12—that the coach work with the coachee to see beyond immediate, superficial problems to issues that are fundamental and systemic.

PRINCIPAL: "Sandy [a teacher] is making me crazy."

COACH: "Tell me about that."

PRINCIPAL: "She is so preoccupied with her personal problems that she is neglecting her students and stepping all over our expectations here."

COACH: "What is your history with this?"

Listen to the coachee's stories and test them. As we have discussed, the ways we behave in the world are shaped by our interpretations of events, the stories we create to explain things. By definition, interpretations are subjective. Interpretations of the past and present shape future actions in ways that may be more or less functional. The fulcrum of transformational coaching is the act of helping a coachee become aware of her interpretations and to explore alternative and more powerful ways of making sense of the world and behaving in relation to it.

PRINCIPAL: "Sandy is a long-time teacher here, and she really does have some difficult personal issues she is dealing with. She was my friend before I even came here, so I know her pretty well. I have talked to her about some of the problems I have observed—being late to class, missing staff meetings, failing to supervise her kids, weak lesson planning—but things don't change."

COACH: "Why do you think things haven't changed?"

PRINCIPAL: "Well, Sandy has a lot going on in her personal life. I don't think that she gets it."

COACH: "Tell me about your communication with her about this."

PRINCIPAL: "It has been frustrating. I try to be supportive. I let her know that I am worried, that as her friend I understand her problems, but that she needs to deal with these school issues."

COACH: "I hear you dealing with this as a personal issue, that you are both concerned and supportive as a friend. Can you imagine tackling this situation from a different role or point of view?"

Use data to shift the coachee's perspective. Data can range from a coach's own observations, to the results of surveys, to research demonstrating that the coachee's conclusions may be incorrect. Each of these can play a critical role in helping a coach challenge a coachee's stories and interpretations.

PRINCIPAL: "I am afraid that if I confront Sandy about these issues, she'll collapse emotionally and the staff will blame me. Many of them really sympathize with Sandy."

COACH: "Let's refer back to that 360° instrument we did with your staff a few months ago. Do you remember what that survey told us about how you are perceived by your staff?"

PRINCIPAL: "Well, they were pretty supportive."

COACH: "Yes, they were. The majority of respondents expressed a high degree of confidence in your leadership. You have a lot of capital with your staff. I recall there were also several comments suggesting that you need to be consistent with students and staff, that sometimes you give different messages to different people."

PRINCIPAL: "I remember that. Maybe I do need to be clearer with Sandy."

Develop and test interpretations and strategies that could help the coachee deal successfully with the breakdown. What is there about the coachee's current way of being that is preventing her from moving forward? What assessments is she making about the situation or herself that are keeping her from taking effective action? What interpretations is the coachee holding that limit her possibilities, and how might they be shifted? Answers to these questions may not be immediately apparent, and a coach should explore alternatives with the coachee, testing out a variety of perspectives that could lead to movement.

COACH: "I have an idea about what might be going on here, and I'd like to share it with you. It has to do with your own identity in this situation. Are you OK with me exploring this with you?"

PRINCIPAL: "Sure."

COACH: "I am wondering if you are having a hard time playing the supervisor role. I know that you value your collegial relationship with your staff and in particular your history of friendship with some people, and I suspect you fear that if you hold Sandy accountable, it will jeopardize those relationships."

PRINCIPAL: "There may be some truth to that . . ."

COACH: "I also suspect that it is not easy for you to play the supervisor role, that you hesitate to be the 'bad guy.'"

PRINCIPAL: "I hate being the bad guy."

Help the coachee construct new interpretations, new stories that open up possibilities for effective action. In *Masterful Coaching*, Robert Hargrove (1995) suggests that coaches help their coachees turn "rut stories into river stories." The first step is for the coach to "recognize and interrupt the rut story" and help the coachee to "understand the nature of the rut story" (p. 65). A rut story is an identity or interpretation of the world that limits possibilities. In this case, our coachee is stuck in the rut of wanting to be seen as humane and collegial. This prevents her from functioning as a supervisor and leader, and therefore from doing the right thing for her school. Hargrove says that once a rut story is named and understood, a coach can work with a coachee to build and practice a "river story," a new interpretation that allows for effective action (pp. 63–65).

Here the coach is beginning to help the coachee explore the possibility that if she holds Sandy accountable, she will be seen as an effective leader rather than as a "bad guy":

COACH: "So, you tell yourself that to be a supervisor, and to hold Sandy accountable, you will have to be the 'bad guy' and that people won't like you as a result."

PRINCIPAL: "There is an element of that in this situation. I am trying to build a positive culture here."

COACH: "What are the consequences of the 'you-as-bad-guy' story?"

PRINCIPAL: "Well, it leaves me pretty paralyzed. Sandy is still doing her thing, and I am kind of conflicted about it."

COACH: "OK, so let's try building a different story. Let's start with the way you would be perceived by staff. Rather than being seen as a bad guy for holding Sandy accountable, is it possible that your actions could be appreciated? What would that look like?"

PRINCIPAL: "I suppose that some staff members are frustrated by having to deal with Sandy's rowdy students in the hallways, and they resent the fact that she misses meetings and such. They might appreciate it if I took this on."

Use hypothetical situations and role playing to help the coachee practice new ways of being. A coaching conversation is an opportunity to test out new interpretations and new ways of being. Mediational questions can lead a coachee to explore new possibilities at the cognitive level and can even lead a coachee to project herself emotionally into an imagined scenario. Situated in the protected space created by the coaching relationship, the coachee can rehearse new ways of being.

COACH: "What would it be like for you to take off your old colleague hat and put on the supervisor/leader hat—and to be very clear with Sandy about your expectations?"

PRINCIPAL: "I've tried that, but I guess I haven't been too effective. I always find myself backing off."

COACH: "So let's do a couple of role plays. In both, I'll play Sandy. In the first, I want you to be the hesitant you. But in the second, put on the supervisor/leader hat."

Create possibilities for the coachee to practice new ways of being in the real world. Transformation happens over time and through practice. Most change of this nature is gradual rather than cathartic. Our principal's growth as a supervisor and leader will occur incrementally, as she gains confidence and experience exercising this new role. It is important to take steps to ensure that commitments made in coaching conversations to exercise new ways of being are fulfilled outside those conversations. Coachees should agree to practice their new learning, and coaches should help them follow through by asking coachees to report back on their experiences during subsequent sessions.

COACH: "How about if right now you develop a plan to meet with Sandy to outline your concerns and to lay out your expectations?"

PRINCIPAL: "OK, I'll ask her to meet with me after tomorrow's staff meeting. I suppose I should start by sharing the problems I've observed, then get real clear about what needs to change."

COACH: "Let's write down specifics of the problems you plan to share with her and what you expect from her in the future."

PRINCIPAL: "I think I'll start with supervision issues. Twice in the last week she has released her students . . ."

(The conversation continues until a concrete plan for the meeting with Sandy is established.)

COACH: "How can I support you with this meeting? I could help you plan it; I could observe it and give you feedback; I could debrief with you after it's over. I can do one, two, or all of these things."

THE RELATIONSHIP OF DISPOSITIONS TO TRANSFORMATIONAL COACHING

Dispositions are the soul of intelligence, without which the understanding and know-how do little good.

David Perkins, author and
founder of Harvard's Project Zero

Imagine a principal with an IQ of 120 who is a master of all the knowledge, skills, and abilities outlined in the ISLLC Standards. This principal has outstanding credentials and years of experience. But he does not really believe, in his heart of hearts, that all students can learn. He does not actually trust or respect teachers. How effective would you expect this imaginary principal to be?

Effective school leaders are fueled by commitments, beliefs, and passions. Michael Fullan (1993) calls this *moral purpose.* We applaud the

Interstate School Leadership Licensure Consortium for deciding to address this issue by including what are called *dispositions* in the Standards. The ISLLC Standards include statements such as "The proposition that diversity enriches the school" (ISLLC, 1996, p. 16) and "The right of every student to a free, quality education" (p. 18).

Here are a few of the 43 statements from the ISLLC Standards (1996) that relate to dispositions:

The administrator believes in, values, and is committed to

- Using the influence of one's office with ethics and integrity in the service of all students and their families
- The proposition that all students can learn
- A school vision of high standards and expectations of learning
- Continuous school improvement
- The proposition that diversity enriches the school
- Collaboration and communication with families, community, students and other stakeholder groups, and their involvement in decision making
- Trusting people and their judgments and involving them in leadership and management processes
- Actively participating in the political and policy-making context in the service of education (pp. 10–21)

The ISLLC Standards suggest that school leaders who do not share these dispositions are not likely to be successful. Principals who are not driven by a sense of moral purpose are not likely to last.

Resource C contains a Dispositions Self-Assessment for use by coaches and coachees. We suggest that coaches use this tool with their coachees and talk explicitly about the core beliefs and commitments that help principals get out of bed every morning and take on their difficult jobs.

We do not mean to imply that a principal must agree passionately with each of the ISLLC dispositions. There is room for difference of opinion in public education. But those principals who are clear about why they are in their profession, and who are fueled by visceral commitments, are the ones who are able to make the greatest difference for kids.

We also want to be very clear in stating that dispositions are not fixed. They shift over time and—for some of us—from hour to hour. When dispositions and their impact upon the principalship are recognized, they can be the subject of learning, coaching, and personal and professional growth. The recognition of and intervention with dispositions fall into the domain of triple-loop learning and transformational coaching.

Let's examine a case study through the lens of the ISLLC dispositions and explore the possibilities for coaching:

Rick is convinced that things are going well at his school, given a low-income community, an inexperienced staff with high turnover, and a high proportion of English Language Learners. The campus is clean and orderly, and morale is generally good. Rick is aware that his students' performance on all measures of achievement is lower than at other schools in the district, but he is resigned to this, believing that students are doing as well as can be expected under the circumstances.

Let's assume that Rick is a hard-working, dedicated principal. But it may be possible that in his heart of hearts, he doesn't believe in, value, or commit to a school vision of high standards of learning, the educability of all, doing the work required for high levels of personal and organizational performance, or taking risks to improve schools (ISLLC, 1996, pp. 10–21).

Is Rick a lost cause? At first glance, perhaps. But like many administrators who tell themselves rut stories about their schools and their students, Rick entered the profession because he wanted to make a difference. The deluge of challenges flooding the public school principalship has doused the fire in his belly. Can a coaching process help to rekindle Rick's passion and bring him to higher levels of expectation and motivation? We believe that it can.

A skilled coach will challenge Rick about his dispositions: What does he really believe his students and school are capable of, and how is he communicating those beliefs? What does he need to experience in order to shift his beliefs? How does his interpretation of the causes of the low level of student achievement at his site prevent him from leading the school forward? What strengths can he build upon in creating a river story, a new interpretation that will open up new possibilities?

To accomplish this, the coach will apply Blended Coaching Strategies when working with Rick. Using an instructional mode, his coach might arrange for him to visit schools with similar demographics and stronger outcomes. Using facilitative and transformational modes, the coach can lead Rick to refine his vision for the school and give him feedback as he works to communicate and implement it. Over time, as Rick awakens to new possibilities and sets higher expectations and experiences incremental success, he just might, in his heart of hearts, commit to a more ambitious set of dispositions.

Reflection: Can you identify a time in your own professional history when your beliefs or dispositions changed in a way that impacted student achievement? Can you identify a "rut story" that leaves you stuck, and can you articulate a "river story" that opens up different possibilities?

Table 11.2   Blended Coaching Strategies

COMPARING INSTRUCTIONAL & FACILITATIVE COACHING STRATEGIES

	INSTRUCTIONAL	FACILITATIVE
Each primarily addresses . . .	ways of doing . . . • *How can we challenge our gifted students?* • *What do I do with all of this student data?*	ways of being . . . • *I get uptight every time I have to meet with the gifted parents.* • *Can we really close the achievement gap?*
and supports the development of . . .	knowledge and skills . . . • *Proven models for differentiation in middle school classrooms* • *Templates for the presentation and analysis of student data*	dispositions and internal capacity . . . • *A passionate belief in the school's obligation to every student* • *Self-reflection and ongoing learning through the process of leading school improvement*
through the exercise of . . .	the basic coaching skills of • Building trust and rapport • Listening • Observing • Questioning • Providing feedback • Summarizing and committing to next steps	
and basic moves such as . . .	• Analyzing the knowledge and skills required to complete a task • Getting permission to instruct • Sharing examples, models, resources, methods and information	• Paraphrasing, clarifying, asking mediational questions • Guiding reflection upon feedback • Examining assertions and assessments • Developing problem solving skills • Shifting the locus of control to the coachee
Particular approaches include but are not limited to . . .	Consultative coaching • The coach shares his/her expertise and may collect and analyze data, outline options, and share suggestions	Transformational coaching • The coach facilitates a processes aimed at producing deep personal transformation in the coachee
	Collaborative coaching • The coach uses both instructional and facilitative approaches as the coach and coachee work together in a master/apprentice relationship to complete a project	
A skillful coach orchestrates a fluid, blended, reiterative process . . .	 **BLENDED COACHING STRATEGIES**	

In Chapters 6 through 11, we have explored the concept of Blended Coaching Strategies as a way of structuring coaching interactions. We suggest that coaches nurture change in a coachee's "ways of doing" and "ways of being" by using both instructional and facilitative coaching strategies. Working from instructional and facilitative stances, coaches may take consultative, collaborative, transformational, or other approaches. Table 11.2 illustrates the relationship between these approaches.

Leadership coaching is a complex process that is often informed by intuition. None of us will become accomplished practitioners by reading a book or attending a workshop. We can learn to be effective coaches, however, by approaching it as we do any challenging discipline, through ongoing practice and feedback from colleagues in our shared professional learning community.

PART III

Using Coaching to Drive School Improvement

In Part I, we outlined the value of leadership coaching as a tool for the professional development of school leaders, and we discussed the basic skills that school leadership coaches should possess. In Part II, we illustrated the application of two fundamental coaching strategies, facilitative and instructional coaching, and uses of collaborative, consultative, and transformational approaches to coaching in a fluid, blended process. Table 11.2 illustrates the ways in which these concepts and practices interact.

In Part III, we bring all of this together through a discussion of the importance of using coaching to drive systems improvement. We discuss the components of quality leadership coaching and professional development induction programs, and we share a variety of resources intended to help individuals and organizations that are interested in building such programs.

12

Coaching for Systems Change

Systems thinking is a body of knowledge and tools that helps us see underlying patterns and how they can be changed. It is these patterns that are roadblocks to change, not specific people or events.

Nancy Isaacson and Jerry Bamburg,
authors and educators

Our work as leadership coaches is about making a difference for students. In order to effect a lasting impact on student achievement, coaches have to help their coachees look beneath and beyond immediate problems to identify systemic causes and opportunities. Let's see what we find when we bring a systems perspective to Jeffers High School, a large urban school, and its principal, Paul:

PAUL: "I'm pretty frustrated with my assistant principals. I have asked them to spend 30 percent of their time in classrooms in order to support teachers in implementing our writing across the curriculum initiative, but I don't see them in the classrooms—and I'm afraid many teachers are blowing off the writing initiative. This is important. We have to raise our passing rate on the exit exam!"

COACH: "Let's focus on your APs for now. What do you think is preventing them from getting into classrooms?"

PAUL: "I'm just not sure if it is a priority for them. I'm not sure they know how to support teachers in teaching writing across the curriculum. What they'll tell you, though, is that they are tied up with discipline and campus supervision."

COACH: "How have you dealt with your APs about this?"

PAUL: "I guess I need to ride them harder about getting into class-rooms. I know they would like me to take things off their plates, but I don't know what that might look like."

At this point, a coach might be tempted to problem solve with Paul about the supervision of his assistant principals, their professional development, and the ways in which their duties are assigned. This approach might tease out some strategies for an incremental change in the ways APs use their time, but it would bypass an opportunity to intervene on a deeper level.

A number of facts emerge as Paul's coach questions him about his APs and their role at Jeffers High School. It turns out that the APs process an average of 9,000 tardies, 900 teacher-generated discipline referrals, 1,200 work detail assignments, and 800 suspensions each year, most of which are for an accumulation of minor offenses such as tardies and dress code violations. Despite the presence of ten classified campus supervisors, the APs are expected to be on the yard at every break as well as before and after school. It's no wonder that the APs have no time to get into classrooms. It's also not a surprise that achievement data for the school are below those for schools with similar populations.

In helping Paul think about why his APs are not getting into classrooms, several deeply systemic issues emerge. These include the need to clarify the role of assistant principals as instructional leaders and to train and support them in exercising the role, the need to transform the school culture from one that pushes out noncompliant students to one that strives to regain their commitment to schooling, and the need to build administrative mechanisms that will reduce the amount of time administrators spend processing discipline issues.

Until the school takes steps to reduce the number of tardies, teacher referrals, suspensions, and work details, the APs will not have time to get into classrooms. Until the school takes on the cultural transformations that result in kids getting into class on time and in all teachers pulling their weight in dealing with discipline, student achievement at Jeffers High will not increase. As long as the school continues to suspend students for failing to dress out for PE, and for accumulating tardies and such, many students will continue to be sucked into the cycles of failure that inevitably result in poor results on the exit exam

COACH (referring to a rough chart he has drawn with Paul):	"So it looks like there are at least 15 significant factors tied to the difficulties that your APs are having getting into classrooms."
PAUL:	"OK, so it's not about me just telling my APs to get into classrooms more often, or just telling my teachers that I expect them to teach the writing curriculum."
COACH:	"I think you're right. It's far more complex than that, and dealing with this complexity offers far bigger payoffs. Where do you think you should go from here?"
PAUL:	"What if we were to have some focus groups with students and teachers to think about ways in which we can reduce tardies and suspensions? And I'm not taking about bringing in just the student council kids."

WHAT ARE SYSTEMS?

There are many systems at play in schools. Some contribute to a school's ability to achieve its goals; some do just the opposite. Some are formal, procedural systems, such as attendance tracking and monitoring. Others are overarching, complex, and informal, as in the relationship between teacher expectations, classroom environment, and student attendance and achievement. Some have been created through deliberate processes, while others have evolved and exist by default. Often, systems are invisible to those who are immersed in them. The coach, as a different observer from outside the institution, can help the coachee to see both deliberate and default systems, to evaluate their impacts, and to explore alternatives.

Systemic considerations such as resource allocation, professional development, and the use of data in decision making have an impact on virtually every aspect of school quality. They overlap and relate to one another synergistically. A school cannot implement an effective system of continuous improvement processes, for example, without also having effective data collection, analysis, and communication systems in place. An effective system of professional development that addresses school needs will be difficult to attain without an effective assessment system and a system for articulating shared beliefs and vision.

What's the difference between an effective process and an effective system? A professional development day in which teachers look at assessment data, identify strengths and weaknesses, and write up and turn in notes can be an isolated procedural event. It can also be part of a larger systemic initiative. Are there guidelines for the data analysis and collaborative processes? Does everyone involved know what the steps and timeline are? Do we know how we will measure our success and how often we will do it? Are there explicit processes in place to connect the examination of data to what happens in the classroom? Was this a one-time event, or can staff say, "We consistently do it this way at our school"? When a school has planned, communicated, and implemented the specific ways processes will work, we can say that a proactive systemic approach is being taken.

AN EXAMPLE OF
COACHING FOR SYSTEMS CHANGE

Lydia approached her coach with a problem. She was not satisfied with attendance at the recent Homewood Elementary Back to School Night and was having trouble getting parents to volunteer for her site council. She was frustrated; she just couldn't think of a way to get more parents to read the flyers that went home with students every week.

Lydia's coach resisted the temptation to help Lydia brainstorm better ways of getting publicity into parents' hands. Instead, the coach helped her recognize that her approach to parent communication had been haphazard. Together they explored the possibility that the school's culture and history of relationships with the community were inhibiting parent engagement. If Lydia was truly interested in increasing parent participation, she needed to develop a plan that went beyond improving parent notification and then implement and evaluate its impact. Lydia and her coach collaborated to come up with the action plan illustrated in Table 12.1.

This plan was implemented, and it began to have an impact on parent attendance at school events. The spring parent survey indicated that some parents felt that home-school communications had improved. However, the percentage of parents attending school events, volunteering, and even responding to the survey did not meet Lydia's expectations. Upon further reflection and conversation with parents, Lydia realized that many parents were not comfortable at the school and did not feel welcomed. The *superficial symptom* of poor parent attendance was the result of a *systemic failure* to create a culture that welcomed and valued parents. At the core of this problem was a teaching staff that had difficulty relating to the new immigrant groups that had moved to the school. Lydia worked with her coach, parents, and staff to implement a number of steps at the classroom, site, and community levels. While these—shown in Table 12.2—were not all directly related to parent attendance at school events, they resulted in much higher levels of participation.

It is easy to focus on surface or presenting problems without ever getting at systemic issues. It is the coach's job to help the coachee get out of the

Table 12.1   Homewood Elementary Parent Publicity Plan

Recurring Need	Procedures and Processes
Parents need timely access to basic calendar information	✓ All communications in English, Spanish, and Vietnamese ✓ Master wall calendar in front office maintained by office manager ✓ Annual calendar mailed to parents in May and September and included in all registration and visitor packets; copies available in office display rack all year long ✓ Monthly newsletter mailed home that includes updated two-month calendar
Parents need timely access to information about schoolwide and special events	✓ All communications in English, Spanish, and Vietnamese ✓ Phone calls and home visits by bilingual liaison to encourage participation by underrepresented families ✓ Monthly newsletter mailed home that includes updated school activities and announcements ✓ Every newsletter includes a *How to Reach Us* section, with phone numbers, school address, Web site, and e-mail addresses ✓ Parent information marquee in front of school maintained and updated weekly by PTA ✓ Glass showcase on outside wall displays current notices for parents and community as well as school events and activities maintained and updated weekly by a staff representative with parent volunteer ✓ Copies of notices, schedules, and flyers displayed on a wall rack accessible to visitors, regularly re-supplied and updated by office assistant ✓ Recording of school events, reminders, and dates available on answering voice mail, updated daily by office assistant ✓ School Web site provides access to all notices and schedules, updated weekly by Tech Coordinator, School Tech Club, and parent volunteers ✓ White board with daily announcements maintained for all staff and parent volunteers; all staff can contribute announcements; office assistant cleans and monitors daily
Trends in parent participation will be measured so this plan can be evaluated and adjusted	✓ Parent evaluation of quality of home-school communication in annual spring survey ✓ Input from site council ✓ Measure trends in parent participation in key events and committees ✓ Measure trends in participation of underrepresented parents

Table 12.2   Systems Interventions at Homewood Elementary

Level	Intervention
Classroom	All home-school communications from classroom teachers translated into home languages
	Full-time translator made available to teachers for calls and conferences
	All teachers have voice mail and stated expectation to return calls within 24 hours
	All classrooms reflect multicultural themes
	Quality of teacher/home communication a focus of the teacher supervision process
	Teachers expected to telephone target parents to encourage attendance at conferences and other key events
Site	Ongoing training and dialogue for all staff around diversity and community issues
	Parent meetings at times determined by parents, with translation and child care
	Purchase of multicultural classroom teaching resources
	Recruitment of teachers and other staff members representative of the community
	Ongoing measurement of parent participation and attitudes
Community	Principal outreach to community groups and churches
	Engagement of diverse community leadership in school improvement processes

habit of "putting out fires" and instead to invest time and energy installing automatic sprinkler systems and removing fuel and sources of ignition.

Table 12.3 provides three more examples—from our own coaching experience—of presenting problems that principals have brought to us, the superficial causes that were the initial focus of our conversations, and the systemic causes that were at the root of the problems.

COACHING FOR SYSTEMS CHANGE AND TIME MANAGEMENT

Most school leaders struggle with time management. The demands of the job seem overwhelming, and the dozens of interactions a school principal must engage in during any one hour make it difficult to take the long view. Steven Covey, author of *Seven Habits of Highly Effective People,* provides a useful frame for thinking about the relationship between leading systems change and managing time. Covey (1989) suggests our time is spent in four kinds of activities, as illustrated in Figure 12.1.

School leaders often become stuck in a cycle of responding to urgent issues, both important and not important. Systems solutions, on the other

Table 12.3   From the Superficial to the Systemic

Issues	Superficial Causes	Systemic Causes
(1) There are currently too many invalid referrals from classroom teachers to the school's Student Study Team (SST).	Staff members are not following the school guidelines for SST referrals.	There is no system for ongoing communication between special education and classroom teachers. Most staff lack a repertoire of differentiation strategies for academic and behavioral interventions. The culture of the school is one in which teachers view "special needs" students as "someone else's responsibility."
(2) The principal is stressed about never having enough time to complete tasks or projects.	She is currently spending 60 minutes a day supervising recesses. She sees five to ten students each day who are sent to the office.	There is an outdated school discipline plan that has no clear system for office referrals. There is no system in place for substitute yard supervision, except default to the principal. The principal does not practice scheduling and prioritizing tasks.
(3) A teacher at the school is not teaching the required English Language Development (ELD) lessons.	The teacher likes to teach physical education and is allotting 40 minutes a day to this subject area. The teacher claims she can't "fit everything in" to the curriculum.	The district lacks an adopted ELD curriculum with a system of assessment. The school has no consistent practice of collaborative curriculum planning and delivery.

hand, are almost never urgent and are almost always important. A critical role for the coach, then, is to help the coachee carve out the time and the psychological space in which to do the important but not urgent work of identifying and implementing the structural interventions that will make a true and lasting difference for students.

Reflection: Review the three examples of problems and systemic issues above. Do you agree that the systemic causes we outline are important but not urgent? Can you think of ways in which the failure to address these systemic issues might produce problems that are urgent?

Figure 12.1   Four Types of Leadership Tasks

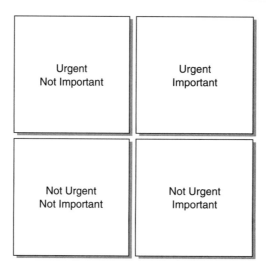

Urgent Not Important	Urgent Important
Not Urgent Not Important	Not Urgent Important

COACHING OUTCOMES

In coaching for systems improvement, the coach helps the coachee to:

- Look behind the presenting problem to the underlying causes of an issue
- Become skilled at identifying systemic problems that surface as minor issues
- Invest in systems improvements rather than short-term solutions

As school administrators gain experience, they recognize systems and become skilled at setting up new systems and tuning up old ones. Yet administrators vary in their ability to recognize and analyze systems. With coaching, principals can become experts at implementing systems that will not only ensure that their schools run smoothly, but that will also provide the time and structures for instructional leadership.

Exercise: Look at Table 12.4. Read over the issues presented by the principal. Reflect on the superficial causes that the principal has assigned to the issues. What deeper systemic causes could be at play?

For each of these cases, imagine the ways in which you could use facilitative strategies to gain a better understanding of systemic causes. What steps could you take using a consultative approach to help you and your

Table 12.4 Consider Underlying Systemic Causes

Issues	Superficial Causes
(1) The school budget is a "mess" with no clear information available for the principal to use in making decisions.	The secretary is new and has no budget experience. The district office budget printouts arrive late and are difficult to interpret.
(2) An influential parent is complaining about a teacher not being accessible for questions, information, and conversations about her child.	The teacher in question does not have a phone in her room. The teacher coaches basketball in the afternoon and says she does not have time to meet with the parent.
(3) For the third year in a row, the target populations (Latino and African American subgroups) have not met their AYP growth target, although there has been a slight increase in their reading and math scores at most grade levels.	High staff turnover has had a negative impact on students at this school. An analysis of attendance data shows a higher rate of absenteeism among African American and Latino students.

coachee have a better understanding of the facts? How could you work either collaboratively or in a facilitative mode to help a principal create and implement an action plan that would address the underlying problems?

In the face of immediate concerns, we often have difficulty "seeing" the systems at play. Systems analysis takes practice, both on the part of the principal and the coach.

Our point in this chapter is a deceptively simple one: the role of a school leadership coach is to try always to move coaching conversations and interventions beyond the immediate issues to those underlying opportunities for systems improvement that are likely to have the greatest positive impact on students.

13

Designing a Leadership Coaching Program

The coach-coachee relationship is at the heart of a coaching-based leadership professional development program. A number of other considerations also impact program quality. These include the selection and professional development of the leadership coach and the structure and curriculum of the coaching process.

WHO SHOULD COACH?

Many hugely successful basketball and football players have tried their hands at coaching, and most of them have had less success as coaches than they did as players. Many first-class coaches were never top-tier players. What does this tell us about the relationship between being a school leader and becoming a school leadership coach?

Qualifications and Selection of Leadership Coaches

One thing is very clear: exceptional school leaders are not necessarily exceptional leadership coaches. An individual who has a stellar reputation and track record as a principal or superintendent may not possess the interpersonal skills and professional knowledge required of a leadership coach. It is critically important that we be conscious of this, because school leadership coaches are frequently drawn from the ranks of retirees. Retirees are a remarkable resource, but potential coaches must be screened to ensure that they are a match for the work, just as they would be in any other high-stakes employment decision.

Must a coach always have experience in the coachee's job? In the private sector, CEOs work with executive coaches who have never served in the top seat. Many athletic coaches have never competed as players at the level of the teams they coach. Because we suggest a dynamic model of coaching that includes instructional strategies, we believe that coaches must have a firm handle on the knowledge and skills required of the individuals they are coaching, but a precise job match is not required. It isn't necessary to have been a high school principal in order to coach a high school principal (although it helps), but one should certainly have a strong grasp of the issues faced by high school leaders and a vision for quality secondary education.

At times, a coach may be called upon to support a leader in a single focus area. In this sort of circumstance, expertise in that focus area (along with coaching skills) may be more important than possessing leadership experience in a role similar to that of the coachee. For instance, a high school principal working to implement writing instruction across the curriculum may benefit from focused coaching by a literacy expert who has never served in a principalship but has extensive experience with professional development at the secondary level.

We suggest that at a minimum, school leadership coaches should meet the following qualifications:

- Five years of successful educational leadership experience;
- Evidence of successful informal mentoring relationships; and
- Evidence of appropriate dispositions, knowledge, and skills.

The selection process should require

- The submission of letters of recommendation that specifically address the ability to serve in a coaching role;
- A formal interview which includes role-playing of coaching scenarios; and
- Reference checks.

Selection as a coach should be conditional upon

- Completion of a training program; and
- Participation in ongoing professional development that includes
  - ✓ Shadowing and being shadowed by an experienced coach, and
  - ✓ Participation in a community of practice that meets regularly to reflect on current issues in serving as coaches.

"Outside" Versus "Inside" Coaches

As we illustrated in Chapter 2, we believe that school leaders need both internal and external supports in order to succeed in today's demanding environment. Ideally, a coach is part of the *external* support system.

An external coach is independent of a coachee's school system. She is able to assure the coachee of confidentiality. Her commitment is to serve the school system (which is usually the paying customer) by dedicating herself to supporting the success of the coachee *outside of the summative evaluation process.* This is particularly important given the political vulnerability of school leaders.

This is not to say that coaches should not be in communication with coachees' supervisors. Regular, three-way conversations among coaches, coachees, and supervisors are important in order to ensure that the professional development focus of the coaching work is aligned with the supervisor's perceptions and expectations.

It is often difficult to establish programs in which coaches are "outsiders." Sometimes it is easiest for school districts to establish their own internal programs of coaching support for principals. Where this is to be the case, it is very important that the role of the coach in relation to the district be clearly defined—and the boundaries of confidentiality be established and maintained.

CAN SUPERVISORS BE COACHES?

In our experience, it is difficult if not impossible for supervisors to provide the kind of intensive leadership coaching we describe in this book. The school principalship is a highly difficult and political job that is subject to intense public scrutiny. It is almost impossible for a subordinate to establish a totally open, vulnerable relationship with a supervisor in this context. School leaders often have their greatest struggles in interfacing with district leaders and systems. A subordinate may be hesitant to seek coaching about maneuvering in a problematic bureaucracy from a boss who represents that bureaucracy. Furthermore, we believe that leadership coaching is most powerful when it is delivered by a professional coach—an individual who has dedicated his or her time and purpose to the practice of coaching.

This is not to say that the skills and strategies we have outlined in this book are not of use to supervisors. Effective supervisors can and do use coaching strategies and skills to support the growth of their subordinates. In fact, with the large majority of subordinates who are competent and who take responsibility for their own performance, the best supervisors work from a coaching stance most of the time. However, the fact that a supervisor can direct, evaluate, hire, and fire trumps even the most trusting coaching relationship between a supervisor and a supervisee.

ONGOING PROFESSIONAL
DEVELOPMENT FOR COACHES

Leadership coaching is a demanding and complex professional practice. Leadership coaches should come to their work well prepared, with the recognition that to be a leadership coach is to be committed to one's own ongoing professional growth. Before serving in a coaching role, coaches should have initial training and experiences in the kinds of skills and strategies outlined in this book. But this background is only a foundation for what should be an ongoing learning process.

School leadership coaches should be engaged in the following activities as integral elements of their practice:

Maintaining Currency in the World of School Improvement. Leadership coaches (who, as we've noted, are often retirees) must stay on top of research, legislation, and current trends in the education community. They can accomplish this through reading, conference attendance, and by staying connected to the daily lives of school leaders.

Seeking Models and Feedback in the Real Work of Coaching. It is extremely valuable for novice coaches to shadow experienced coaches and to be observed by them as they coach. It should be our goal to build apprenticeship relationships that naturally evolve into collegial ones.

Acquiring New Approaches to Coaching. There is a good deal of literature and a vast professional development community concerned with executive coaching, particularly in the private sector. We encourage school leadership coaches to explore these resources.

Participating in Communities of Practice. It is essential that leadership coaches build communities of practice for one another. Such communities become places for shared problem solving, for the learning and application of new strategies and skills, and for the general strengthening of professional practice.

Committing to Reflective Practice. Leadership coaches need to exercise the self-discipline of examining and reflecting on their daily practice. They should solicit feedback from those they serve and make time to unpack their self-observations. A journal can be a highly effective tool for this purpose.

FORMATIVE ASSESSMENT AS A
FRAMEWORK FOR LEADERSHIP DEVELOPMENT

Effective professional development is organized around outcomes and therefore demands a clear understanding of the skills, knowledge, and dispositions we are trying to produce. The ISLLC Standards articulate the

Figure 13.1   The Formative Assessment Cycle

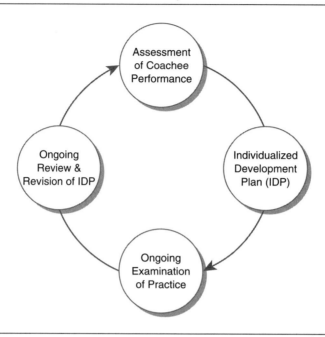

vision on which our coaching is centered. It is the coach's job to help the coachee grow into the school leader described by the ISLLC Standards.

Formative assessment is a continuous improvement cycle, one led by the coach but owned by the coachee. The cycle begins by taking stock of the coachee's context, needs, strengths, and weaknesses. Resource A contains a sample tool for this purpose, a self-reflection assessment guide that can be completed by the coachee, the supervisor, the coach, and others. This guide is derived from the ISLLC Standards. Other tools in the Resources section include a 360° survey instrument to gather perceptual data from subordinates and others. These might include prior years' evaluations, school data, and anything else that will help to identify a coachee's strengths and areas for growth as well as establish leadership priorities in the coachee's context.

Leadership coaching should be organized around the accomplishment of explicit goals, goals that are aligned with ISLLC Standards and informed by contextual data. Specific plans should be made to achieve them. One tool for this purpose is the Individualized Development Plan (IDP) shown in Figure 13.2 and included in Resource C.

The IDP—negotiated between coach and coachee—outlines the key steps each will take and sets out a specific plan to achieve explicit goals. It is usually developed annually and is regularly revisited and revised. Present throughout the coaching process, it provides a focal point for ongoing examination of practice.

Figure 13.2   Individualized Development Plan

INDIVIDUALIZED   DEVELOPMENT   PLAN   (IDP)

STANDARD:		COACHEE	
		COACH	
ELEMENT OF THE STANDARD:		SUPERVISOR	

ACTIVITIES	PERSONS RESPONSIBLE	TIMELINE												EVALUATION	DATE OF REFLECTION INQUIRY MEETING
		JUL	AUG	SEPT	OCT	NOV	DEC	JAN	FEB	MAR	APR	MAY	JUN		

I approve and will support the implementation of the IDP.

COACHEE	Date
COACH	Date
SUPERVISOR	Date

The IDP and the formative assessment process are distinct but not isolated from the process of formal, employer-based summative evaluation. Ideally, the summative evaluation process is organized around the same set of standards that form the basis for formative assessment, and the goals established in the IDP constitute the coachee's professional development goals for the purposes of summative evaluation. The coachee's supervisor participates in the formative assessment and IDP process, and evidence of progress through that process is considered in the summative evaluation. A coach might contribute to the summative evaluation process through a three-way conversation with the supervisor and coachee, discussing the year's activities and accomplishments. An external coach would not, however, share assessments about a coachee's performance with a supervisor.

We suggest that coaches use a Collaborative Log form—illustrated in Figure 13.3 and also included in the Resources section—at every coaching session, as a tool for organizing the coaching process, encouraging accountability on the parts of both the coach and coachee, and maintaining a record of coachee progress. The Collaborative Log is a simple form that brings discipline to the coaching process. Used in conjunction with standards assessment and the IDP, it brings continuity and coherence to the coaching relationship.

Figure 13.3 Collaborative Log

CANDIDATE: _____

MENTOR: _____

| COLLABORATIVE LOG |

DATE: _____

SCHOOL: _____

☐ What's Working?

☐ Current Focus, Challenges, Concerns

☐ Coachee's Next Steps

☐ Coach's Next Steps

☐ Next Meeting Date

☐ Next Meeting Agenda

- Facilitating a Vision of Learning
- Shaping the School Culture and Instructional Program
- Managing the Organization

- Collaborating with Families and Communities
- Modeling Ethics and Building Leadership Capacity
- Responsding to the Political, Social, Economic, Legal & Cultural Context

NEW TEACHER CENTER @ UCSC; used with permission.

Conclusion

I really think I am making a difference here, and you have helped me to make that difference.

I had no idea what I was getting into; I wouldn't have made it without you.

I want a coach for the rest of my career. This is the way I learn!

These are a just a few of the representative comments we've heard from the many individuals we've had the privilege to coach. Our daily work as school leadership coaches offers us the opportunity to interact with some of the most dedicated, passionate, and hard-working people on the planet. They do the toughest and most important work imaginable.

However, it is unfortunately true that most school leaders do not have access to a professional leadership coach. Some individuals are able to succeed in what has been an isolated, sink-or-swim profession despite weak preservice and inservice professional development. Others, by accident or by design, cobble together a functional support system.

Our experience tells us that the work of coaching school leaders is not easy. It is both risky and complex, but it is worth the investment in energy and commitment, in time and training. Our research indicates that school leaders who have the benefit of quality leadership coaching are more likely to have a positive impact on student achievement than school leaders lacking such support.

It is time to invest in coaching-based professional development for school leaders. In this book we have laid the groundwork for the establishment of what we believe is a distinct professional niche in the education community. School leadership coaching is making a difference for our schools, our kids, and our society. We welcome you to this important work, and we invite you to join us in what we hope will be a vibrant learning community of committed and professional school leadership coaches.

LEADERSHIP COACHING RESOURCES

The additional resource materials in this section are organized into three sections, as follows:

A. Materials for Coach Professional Development

A.1. Bias Worksheet. This worksheet is a self-reflection tool for coaches. It is intended to help you understand how your experiences and perspectives impact the way you perceive and behave in the world and how they might affect your coaching practice.

A.2. Assessments Self-Reflection. In Chapter 4 we introduced the distinction between assertions and assessments and the notion that poorly formed assessments can limit our possibilities. This self-reflection is designed to help coaches and others examine the assessments they make about themselves.

A.3. Coaching Feedback. This is one example of the kind of simple tool that should be used by coaches and coaching programs to solicit feedback from coachees in order to strengthen the continual improvement processes of both coaches and programs.

A.4. Ethics for Coaches. This document outlines ethical standards for coaching practice.

B. Establishing the Coaching Relationship

B.1. Making the Most of the Coaching Relationship. This handout lets new coachees know what to expect and encourages them to invest in the coaching relationship. Consider sharing this document with coachees and their supervisors.

B.2. Coaching Agreement. This is a sample contract between coach and coachee, outlining the responsibilities of each party. We suggest that this document or one like it be discussed and signed early in the coaching relationship.

C. Formative Assessment Tools

C.1. Standards-Based Assessment. A coachee, coach, and supervisor can use this sort of tool to assess a coachee's strengths and needs in relation to standards. This can be used as a formative tool—for the purpose of informing the creation of a professional development plan such as the Individual Development Plan that follows—and as a summative assessment.

C.2. Dispositions Self-Assessment. Coaches and coachees may want to use this self-assessment as a tool for reflecting upon their personal beliefs in relation to the dispositions called for in the ISLLC Standards, from which it is derived.

C.3. 360° Survey. Surveys such as this 360° instrument are immensely valuable to coaches and coachees for gathering perceptual data. We recommend that all leaders use a 360° instrument annually and that leadership coaches use the instrument as a primary source for determining the focus of the coaching process.

C.4. Individual Development Plan (IDP). This is a template for an annual professional development plan tied to the ISLLC Standards. In a coherent coaching-based professional development program, such a plan guides coaching and other professional development activities and is tied to the district's evaluation system.

C.5. Collaborative Log. We suggest that this Collaborative Log serve as an organizer and a record for each coaching session. It is completed collaboratively, and both the coach and coachee keep copies.

Resource A: Materials for Coaches

A.1. BIAS WORKSHEET

This worksheet is a self-reflection tool for coaches. It is intended to help you understand how your experiences and perspectives impact the way you perceive and behave in the world and how they might affect your coaching practice.

What are the key factors of your personal background that shape the way you see the world?

Gender	Family Background
Culture	Professional Experience
Personal Style	Race/Ethnicity

A.2. ASSESSMENTS SELF-REFLECTION

In Chapter 4 we introduced the distinction between assertions and assessments and the notion that poorly formed assessments can limit our possibilities. This self-reflection is designed to help coaches and others examine the assessments they make about themselves.

(1) Quickly brainstorm words that describe positive (+) or negative (−) assessments you make about yourself:

(+) Assessment	(−) Assessment

(2) Circle one of the positive assessments you wrote above. What assertions can you make to ground that assessment?

(3) Circle one negative assessment. What assertions can you make to ground that assessment?

(4) What assertions can you make that do not support the negative assessment?

(5) What different assessment would open more possibilities for you?

A.3. COACHING FEEDBACK

This is one example of the kind of simple tool that should be used by coaches and coaching programs to solicit feedback from coachees in order to strengthen the continual improvement processes of both coaches and programs.

Feedback for Coaches

To: _____   Date: _____

In what areas of your principalship are you feeling most successful?	What are your greatest concerns and challenges?
What coaching strategies do I use that are most helpful to you?	What additional ideas or suggestions do you have to help me be a better coach?

A.4. ETHICS FOR COACHES

This document outlines ethical standards for coaching practice.

Code of Ethics for Leadership Coaches

- ✓ I will conduct myself in a manner that serves the goal of doing what is best for students.

- ✓ I will coach my client with the goal of supporting the development of leadership aligned with accepted professional standards.

- ✓ I will build trust in my coaching relationships by consistently being sincere in my communication, reliable in meeting my commitments, and by operating within my areas of competence.

- ✓ I will, at the beginning of each coaching relationship, ensure that my coaching client understands the terms of the coaching agreement between us.

- ✓ I will respect the confidentiality of my client's information, except as otherwise authorized by my client, or as required by law.

- ✓ I will coordinate with and support the goals of my client's employer, while guarding confidentiality and nurturing collaboration between all parties.

- ✓ I will be alert to noticing when my client is no longer benefiting from our coaching relationship and thus would be better served by another coach or by another resource and, at that time, I will encourage my client to make that change.

- ✓ I will avoid conflicts between my interests and the interests of my clients. Whenever the potential for a conflict of interest arises, I will discuss the conflict with my client to reach agreement with my client on how to deal with it in whatever way best serves my client.

Resource B: Establishing the Coaching Relationship

B.1. MAKING THE MOST OF THE COACHING RELATIONSHIP

This handout lets new coachees know what to expect and encourages them to invest in the coaching relationship. Consider sharing this document with coachees and their supervisors.

Making the Most of Coaching

Masterful coaches inspire people by helping them recognize the previously unseen possibilities that lay embedded in their existing circumstances.

Robert Hargrove, author of *Masterful Coaching*

The purpose of this document is to provide you with some basic information that will help you make the most of leadership coaching. If you have additional questions, be sure to share them with your coach.

What is school leadership coaching? Coaching is a one-to-one process for the purpose of helping you clarify your professional goals and achieve them. The ultimate goal of the process is to have a positive impact upon student achievement through the exercise of school leadership. Your coach will use a variety of strategies to support your learning. At times your coach will play an instructional role, serving as a personal teacher, consultant, and collaborator. Often, your coach will take what we call a *facilitative* approach, stimulating your learning through questioning, by providing you with feedback, helping you to analyze your perceptions and behaviors, and guiding you as you experiment with new ways of doing things. Unlike many other professional development models, your coach is there to meet your individual needs.

What kinds of things will we do in coaching? You and your coach will meet regularly, and every session will differ. Much of your time will be spent in conversation, but it is also important that your coach have the opportunity to observe you interacting with people at your site and doing real work. You and your coach may also decide to use survey instruments and other data sources to gather feedback and information to use in the coaching process.

Are these sessions confidential? The principalship is a highly sensitive, demanding, and political position, and confidentiality is critical to the success of coaching. Your coach's commitment is to confidentiality. Aside from sharing general descriptions of the type of work you are doing, your coach will not discuss your coaching relationship with anyone, including your supervisor, without your agreement.

Is coaching a remedial process? Absolutely not. Top athletes, business leaders, and school leaders take advantage of coaching as an important tool for professional growth. Teachers appreciate that principals participating in coaching are modeling lifelong learning for their staffs.

How can I make the most of coaching? Coaching is not a passive process, and the benefits you gain from coaching will be influenced by the degree to which you take advantage of the process. Here are some of the most important things you can do to make the most of coaching:

- ✓ Build uninterrupted time into your schedule for coaching.
- ✓ Take initiative in asking your coach to observe you in difficult situations.
- ✓ Be forthcoming about your problems, doubts, and toughest issues. Let it all hang out.
- ✓ Be willing to take risks with your coach in dealing with uncomfortable topics and in experimenting with uncomfortable solutions.
- ✓ Between coaching sessions, keep track of goals and action plans you have established with your coach.
- ✓ Between coaching sessions, note issues and concerns that might be fruitful to discuss with your coach.
- ✓ Be forthcoming with your coach about anything your coach is doing that is interfering with your ability to get the most out of the relationship.

Congratulations and thanks for taking on some of the most important work in the world, the work of school leadership.

B.2. COACHING AGREEMENT

This is a sample contract between coach and coachee, outlining the responsibilities of each party. We suggest that this document or one like it be discussed and signed early in the coaching relationship.

Sample Coaching Agreement

Coach agrees

- To honor the confidentiality of work with Participant
- To provide one-on-one support to Participant for a minimum of three hours per month
- To utilize proven coaching approaches in work with Participant
- To serve as a support to Participant when possible by securing information, contacts, and other resources as requested and as appropriate
- To respond to Participant in a timely manner between coaching sessions via telephone or e-mail
- To honor the demanding schedule of site administrators, offering services on site whenever possible and avoiding duplication of programs and commitments
- To convene and facilitate occasional job-alike and topical gatherings of program participants
- To commit to supporting the success and effectiveness of Participant as the primary focus and purpose of the program

Participant agrees

- To fully avail him/herself of the support offered by the Coach
- To work with the Coach to identify meaningful goals for the program, in concert with the development of individual goals as required by the Participant's school district
- To approach the coaching relationship with openness and honesty
- To arrange for observations of real-work situations that will allow for targeted coaching, to include at a minimum:

    ✓ A teacher observation cycle
    ✓ Development of a teacher development case study
    ✓ Facilitation of a staff or site council meeting

- To participate in the evaluation of the program and to contribute ideas to the design and revision of the program
- To take full advantage of written materials and other resources made available by the program
- To participate in three off-site meetings during the course of the school year

Participant: _____

Coach: _____

Date: _____

Resource C: Formative Assessment Tools

C.1. STANDARDS-BASED ASSESSMENT

A coachee, coach, and supervisor can use this sort of tool to assess a coachee's strengths and needs in relation to standards. This can be used as a formative tool—for the purpose of informing the creation of a professional development plan such as the Individual Development Plan that follows—and as a summative assessment.

Self-Assessment of Skills in Relation to the ISLLC Standards

A school administrator is an educational leader who promotes the success of all students by . . .	What successes have you experienced this year?	What challenges do you still face?	What professional development needs do you have?
(1) Facilitating the development, articulation, implementation, and stewardship of a vision of learning that is shared and supported by the school community.			
(2) Advocating, nurturing, and sustaining a school culture and instructional program conducive to student learning and staff professional growth.			
(3) Ensuring management of the organization, operations, and resources for a safe, efficient, and effective learning environment.			
(4) Collaborating with families and community members, responding to diverse community needs, and mobilizing community resources.			
(5) Modeling a personal code of ethics and developing professional leadership capacity.			
(6) Understanding, responding to, and influencing the larger political, social, economic, legal, and cultural context.			

C.2. DISPOSITIONS SELF-ASSESSMENT

Coaches and coachees may want to use this self-assessment as a tool for reflecting upon their personal beliefs in relation to the dispositions called for in the ISLLC Standards, from which it is derived.

Dispositions Self-Assessment (Derived from ISLLC Standards)

To what degree do you believe in, value, and commit yourself to . . .	Not at all	Somewhat	Mind, heart, & soul
Student learning as the fundamental purpose of schooling			
The ideal of the common good and the principles of the Bill of Rights			
The right of every student to a free, quality education			
Education as key to social mobility and democracy			
Using the influence of one's office with ethics and integrity in the service of all students and their families			
A safe and supportive learning environment			
The proposition that all students can learn			
A school vision of high standards and expectations of learning			
Continuous school improvement			
The proposition that diversity enriches the school			
Collaboration and communication with families, community, students, and other stakeholder groups and their involvement in decision making			
Ensuring that students have the knowledge, skills, and values needed to become successful adults			
A willingness to continuously examine one's own assumptions, beliefs, and practices			
Doing the work and taking the responsibility required for high levels of personal and organizational performance			
Lifelong learning for self and others			
Professional development as an integral part of school improvement			
The proposition that families have the best interests of their children in mind			
Preparing students to become contributing members of society			
Taking risks to improve schools			
Trusting people and their judgments and involving them in leadership and management processes			
Actively participating in the political and policymaking context in the service of education			

C.3. 360° SURVEY

Surveys such as this 360° instrument are immensely valuable to coaches and coachees for gathering perceptual data. We recommend that all leaders use a 360° instrument annually and that leadership coaches use the instrument as a primary source for determining the focus of the coaching process.

Sample 360° Leadership Survey

Name of Principal_____

Your role _____

Please rate the principal's effectiveness in each area by placing an **x** along the continuum of development from **Beginning** to **Accomplished**. Your specific comments and suggestions will be particularly helpful.

Beginning	Accomplished
← ————————————————————————————→	
ENSURES THE SAFE, EFFICIENT, AND EFFECTIVE MANAGEMENT OF THE SCHOOL	
(Sustains a safe, well-maintained learning environment for students and staff)	
(Effectively manages student discipline policies and procedures)	
(Provides the necessary resources to support the learning of all students)	
COMMENTS and/or SUGGESTIONS	

Beginning	Accomplished

←――――――――――――――――――――――――――――――――→

**FACILITATES THE DEVELOPMENT OF
A VISION OF LEARNING THAT IS SHARED
AND SUPPORTED BY THE SCHOOL COMMUNITY**

**(Promotes a vision of student achievement based
upon data from multiple measures of student learning)**

**(Shapes and coordinates school programs to ensure
they are well communicated and consistent with the vision)**

(Effectively builds buy-in within the entire school community)

COMMENTS and/or SUGGESTIONS

Beginning	Accomplished

$\longleftrightarrow$

**BUILDS AND SUSTAINS A SCHOOL CULTURE AND
INSTRUCTIONAL PROGRAM CONDUCIVE TO STUDENT
LEARNING AND STAFF PROFESSIONAL GROWTH**

**(Promotes equity, fairness, and respect
among all members of the school community)**

**(Shapes a culture of high expectations,
built upon a system of standards-based accountability)**

**(Provides opportunities for all members
of the school community to collaborate,
share responsibility, and exercise leadership)**

COMMENTS and/or SUGGESTIONS

Beginning   Accomplished

←——→

**BUILDS AND SUSTAINS A SCHOOL CULTURE AND
INSTRUCTIONAL PROGRAM CONDUCIVE TO STUDENT
LEARNING AND STAFF PROFESSIONAL GROWTH**

**(Promotes equity, fairness, and respect
among all members of the school community)**

**(Shapes a culture of high expectations,
built upon a system of standards-based accountability)**

**(Provides opportunities for all members
of the school community to collaborate,
share responsibility, and exercise leadership)**

COMMENTS and/or SUGGESTIONS

Beginning	Accomplished

← ———————————————————————————————————— →

**MODELS EFFECTIVE PROFESSIONAL LEADERSHIP,
INTERPERSONAL SKILLS, ETHICS, AND INTEGRITY**

**(Demonstrates skills in decision making,
problem-solving, change management,
conflict resolution, planning, and evaluation)**

**(Encourages and inspires others to
higher levels of performance and motivation)**

(Builds and maintains effective interpersonal relationships)

**(Demonstrates knowledge of curriculum
and ability to be an instructional leader)**

**(Models personal and professional
ethics, integrity, and fairness)**

COMMENTS and/or SUGGESTIONS

Beginning	Accomplished

←————————————————————————————————————→

**UNDERSTANDS AND ENGAGES
WITH IMPORTANT ISSUES BEYOND THE SITE LEVEL**

(Works with central office and the school
board to influence policies that benefit students)

(Ensures that the school complies
with federal, state, and district requirements)

(Views him/herself as a leader of a team
and as a member of a larger team)

COMMENTS and/or SUGGESTIONS

C.4. INDIVIDUAL DEVELOPMENT PLAN (IDP)

This is a template for an annual professional development plan tied to the ISLLC Standards. In a coherent coaching-based professional development program, such a plan guides coaching and other professional development activities and is tied to the district's evaluation system.

INDIVIDUALIZED DEVELOPMENT PLAN (IDP)

STANDARD: _____   COACHEE _____

COACH _____

ELEMENT OF THE STANDARD: _____   SUPERVISOR _____

ACTIVITIES	PERSONS RESPONSIBLE	TIMELINE JUL AUG SEPT OCT NOV DEC JAN FEB MAR APR MAY JUN	EVALUATION	DATE OF REFLECTION INQUIRY MEETING

I approve and will support the implementation of the IDP.

_____ COACHEE   _____ Date

_____ COACH   _____ Date

_____ SUPERVISOR   _____ Date

C.5. COLLABORATIVE LOG

We suggest that this Collaborative Log serve as an organizer and a record for each coaching session. It is completed collaboratively, and both the coach and coachee keep copies.

CANDIDATE: _____

MENTOR: _____

DATE: _____

SCHOOL: _____

COLLABORATIVE LOG	

☐ What's Working?	☐ Current Focus, Challenges, Concerns
☐ Coachee's Next Steps	☐ Coach's Next Steps
☐ Next Meeting Date	☐ Next Meeting Agenda

- Facilitating a Vision of Learning
- Shaping the School Culture and Instructional Program
- Managing the Organization

- Collaborating with Families and Communities
- Modeling Ethics and Building Leadership Capacity
- Responsding to the Political, Social, Economic, Legal & Cultural Context

NEW TEACHER CENTER @ UCSC; used with permission.

References

Block, P. (2000). *Flawless consulting*. San Francisco: Jossey-Bass.

Brooks, M. (1989). *Instant rapport*. New York: Warner Books.

Brounstein, M. (2000). *Coaching and mentoring for dummies*. Foster City, CA: IDG Books.

Costa, A. L., & Garmston, R. J. (2002). *Cognitive coaching: A foundation for renaissance schools*. Norwood, MA: Christopher-Gordon.

Covey, S. (1989). *Seven habits of highly effective people*. New York: Simon & Schuster.

Echeverría, R. O. (1990). Assertions and assessments. In *Mastering the art of professional coaching* (§2, pp. 1–11). San Francisco: The Newfield Group.

Echeverría, R. O., & Olalla, J. (1992). The art of ontological coaching. In *Mastering the art of ontological coaching* (§12, pp. 1–21). San Francisco: The Newfield Group.

Efran, J., & Lukens, M. D. (1985, May-June). The world according to Humberto Maturana. *Networker*, 23–43.

Ekman, P. (2003). *Emotions revealed*. New York: Holt.

Farkas, S., Johnson, J., Duffett, A., & Foleno, T. (with Foley, P.). (2001). *Trying to stay ahead of the game: Superintendents and principals talk about school leadership*. New York: Public Agenda.

Feiman-Nemser, S., & Remillard, J. (1995). *Perspectives on learning to teach*. East Lansing, MI: Michigan State University, National Center for Research on Teacher Learning.

Fullan, M. (1993). *Change forces*. London: Falmer.

Fullan, M. (1997). *What's worth fighting for in the principalship?* New York: Teachers College Press.

Gilley, J. W., & Broughton, N. W. (1996). *Stop managing, start coaching! How performance coaching can enhance commitment and improve productivity*. New York: McGraw-Hill.

Goleman, D. (1998). *Working with emotional intelligence*. New York: Bantam Books.

Goleman, D., Boyatzis, R., & McKee, A. (2002). *Primal leadership: Realizing the power of emotional intelligence*. Boston: Harvard Business School Press.

Hargrove, R. (1995). *Masterful coaching: Extraordinary results by impacting people and the way they think and work together*. San Francisco: Jossey-Bass.

ISLLC. (1996). *Interstate School Leaders Licensure Consortium: Standards for school leaders*. Washington, DC: Council of Chief State School Officers.

Isaacson, N., & Bamburg, J. (1992, November). Can schools become better learning organizations? *Educational Leadership*, 42–44.

Jackson, P. (1995). *Sacred hoops.* New York: Hyperion.

Kouzes, J. P., & Posner, B. (1987). *The leadership challenge.* San Francisco: Jossey-Bass.

Lindsey, R., Robins, K., & Terrell, R. (1999). *Cultural proficiency: A manual for school leaders.* Thousand Oaks, CA: Corwin Press.

McLagan, P., & Krembs, P. (1995). *On the level: Performance communication that works.* San Francisco: Berret-Koehler.

Mehrabian, A. (1972). *Nonverbal communication.* Chicago: Aldine-Atherton.

Perkins, D. (1995). *Outsmarting I.Q.: The emerging science of learnable intelligence.* New York: The Free Press.

Searle, J. R. (1969). *Speech acts.* Cambridge: Cambridge University Press.

Senge, P. M. (1990). *The fifth discipline.* New York: Doubleday.

Speck, M., & Knipe, C. (2001). *Why can't we get it right?: Professional development in our schools.* Thousand Oaks, CA: Corwin Press.

Note: The authors suggest to the reader that the following document, while not directly cited in this book, is an important source of information about school leaders: *The Principal, Keystone of a High Achieving School: Attracting and Keeping the Leaders We Need.* (2000). Arlington, VA: published jointly by the National Association of Elementary School Principals and the National Association of Secondary School Principals.

Index

NOTE: Page numbers in italics indicate figures and illustrations.

Index

NOTE: Page numbers in italics indicate figures and illustrations.

**CORWIN
PRESS**

The Corwin Press logo—a raven striding across an open book—represents the union of courage and learning. Corwin Press is committed to improving education for all learners by publishing books and other professional development resources for those serving the field of K–12 education. By providing practical, hands-on materials, Corwin Press continues to carry out the promise of its motto: **"Helping Educators Do Their Work Better."**